DUTY SHOES

A NURSE'S MEMOIR

Camille Foshee-Mason, RN

Duty Shoes

©2014 By Camille Foshee-Mason
Edited by: Kim Ridley
All rights reserved.

ISBN-13: 978-1497433502
ISBN-10: 1497433509
Also available in eBook publication

Cover Graphics: Elizabeth E. Little, hyliian.deviantart.com
Interior Formatting: The Author's Mentor
www.littleronipublishers.com

PUBLISHED IN THE UNITED STATES OF AMERICA

Dedicated to My Nursing Instructors

Mrs. Sarah Conkle
Mrs. Mary Culberson
Mrs. Kay DeCoudres
Mrs. Susan Kilgore
Mrs. Lena Leverette
Mrs. Joyce Merkle
Mrs. Lillian Mims
Mrs. Thelma Moore
Mrs. Connie Lou Spradley
Mrs. Judy Thomlin
Mrs. Sandra Thompson
Miss Wilma Thompson
Mrs. Dot Vincent

Duty Shoes is a heartwarming memoir of a nursing career filled with caring and service. I laughed and cried with Camille while reading about her experiences. Although the delivery of healthcare has advanced, all nurses can identify with the challenges of nursing and the diversity of our patients. Every nurse and nursing student will enjoy these great stories that give life to the phrase "the heart of nursing."

Marilyn K. Rhodes, EdD, RN, CNM, CNE
COLONEL (ret), USAF, NC

What is written in this volume describes the fascination of one branch of medicine by an RN who chose it as her career. Obstetrics is one discipline involving two patients-one screaming initially and, hopefully, the other screaming incessantly! A joyful noise! A description of the road to this most satisfying status- the OB.RN- is given by this author who is a fine example of her craft.

D. L. Angle, MD

A very enjoyable read! It brought back many memories, especially from when I worked a surgical floor and those early years in OB when we used IV alcohol for preterm labor. Didn't really want to put it down.

Vicki F Brooks, CNM, MPH

A perfect read for anyone in the medical profession. Camille Mason's book allows the reader to follow her throughout her career in one of the world's most selfless and caring professions. *Duty Shoes* is a delightful journey sure to elicit a vast array of emotional responses. Although changes in medicine throughout her career are discussed, a solitary concept remains: the pure joy and triumph of the human spirit.

John Aldridge C.R.N.P.

Foreword

Entering the world of nursing is the beginning of a complex, multi-faceted journey that requires lifelong learning. Nursing is a demanding profession because of the serious nature of the work, an exhausting work schedule, the need to juggle many tasks simultaneously, and the amount of knowledge and cognitive abilities necessary to insure a safe practice. Only those with courage and conviction will be successful.

Camille Mason has written an interesting descriptive account of her nursing journey beginning with her days as a student nurse, continuing with her varied nursing job experiences, and culminating with her present position. Her reflections through those lived experiences demonstrate the many stresses and rewards of a nursing career.

This book offers something for everyone from the beginning nursing student to individuals who have been practicing nurses for many years. There is no doubt every nurse can remember moments from their own journey when they were inspired by a teacher, a friend, a patient, or a coworker and other times when they felt hopeless and powerless by a situation, patient, coworker, or friend. Mrs. Mason has described some of these moments in this book to energize the reader's healing touch. The reader may see similarities with their own journey and understand they are not alone. Through her reflections of her journey, the reader can easily follow the development of attitude, professionalism, and caring which are all hallmarks of a true nurse.

I think we can all agree the process of becoming a nurse and the life of a nurse is a challenge not forgotten by anyone who has bravely undertaken the journey. It is probably one of the most difficult things a person will do in their life, but is a highly rewarding career guaranteed to be worth it. Mrs. Mason's rich collection of her experiences promises to inform and inspire you to continue your journey.

Duty Shoes: A Nurse's Memoir offers you benefits depending on where you are in your journey. If you are a student, it offers a look at the profession you have chosen with the good and bad exposed. If you are an experienced nurse, you will be reminded of some of your own memories that have occurred along your journey. If you are a retiring nurse, then you can reflect over your career for similarities and differences. What they all have in common is a love for nursing and a desire to help their patients and nursing to achieve their full potential. I enjoyed the book and found it valuable. I think you will, too. Enjoy!

Barbara Wilder, PhD, CRNP
Professor
Auburn University School of Nursing
February 7, 2014

☞◦⊰

I shared in many of the early experiences you will read about in this book. I was one of those young female nursing students who assembled in that big room, early September 1973, Camille referenced in her first paragraph. Those first few chapters were certainly a trip down memory lane; many of Camille's memories of nursing school and dorm life are also mine. We were in the same class, lived on the same hall, and were good friends while in school. In retrospect, details of what she experienced are somewhat blurred with my own experiences because we were all right there together. If I didn't live the experience, I certainly heard about it soon after from Camille or another student. All those memories were relived as I read through those opening chapters. Yet, our memories are probably very similar to those of all nurses of our generation.

Duty Shoes is a book every nursing student and nurse should read. Over the years, I've often had nursing colleagues exclaim, I'm going to write a book about what I've seen. So when Camille first told me about her book, I thought, sure, I'll believe it when I see it. But, when I read those opening chapters, I quickly realized the value of Camille's memoir as a wonderful history of the changes in nursing over the last forty years, and as a teaching tool for nursing students. The book provides a delightful account of Camille's nursing journey and an excellent portrayal of "real nursing." When we were in our diploma program, we often heard: "those who can—do; those who cannot—teach." As you read *Duty Shoes*, you will readily recognize Camille as one of those who "can."

I also thought of myself as a doer and was recognized at our graduation with the Florence Nightingale Award for Clinical Proficiency. Life takes funny twists, and I moved from my small rural community to the city so I could continue my nursing education. But through all of the years of education, I remember more from that diploma program and it definitely influenced my clinical practice and my teaching philosophy. As a nurse educator, I've certainly gained greater appreciation for the role our diploma program nursing instructors had in molding us into the nurses we are today. I worked as an adjunct clinical instructor for a few years when my children were young, and I recall taking baccalaureate nursing students to a nursing unit for their first clinical experience. What an eye-opening experience for the students and for me. But, I remembered so much about the way my fundamental's instructor taught us and I used those same principles with my students. In retrospect, the patience and commitment our nursing faculty demonstrated as they taught us how to "be a nurse" certainly are worthy of the dedication Camille gives at the beginning of this book.

Although nursing education has undergone many changes as we transitioned from predominately hospital-based diploma programs to the current movement of eighty percent of all RNs will be BSN prepared by 2020, much is still the same. We joked about the knitted uterus used to demonstrate how the baby moved through the birth canal. But, we always showed respect to our instructors even when we were not doing exactly what they intended. For example, in our quarter for psych nursing, we knew better than to submit our clinical notes with "my patient wouldn't talk to me." The main purpose for psych clinical was to establish a therapeutic relationship with our patient and our instructor expected us to document our communication. Yet, sometimes patients just would not talk so we made up our notes and turned in beautiful, well written notes about our wonderful conversations. But, we learned so much as we looked in our book to find exactly what "the nurse" was supposed to say to the patient. I'm sure our instructor knew there was no way we could have been so eloquent in our "therapeutic communications." Today, nursing education relies very heavily on simulated learning experiences and role playing by nursing students. Little did we know at the time, but we were doing some of the same things in our nursing program.

In reality, diploma nursing programs provided a tremendous immersion into nursing practice which few students get today. Of course, over the last forty years, the explosion of nursing knowledge is beyond comprehension and nursing programs cannot possibly teach everything a nurse needs in today's health care settings. To address all these changes, more hospitals are providing a three-to-six month internship or residency program for new graduate hires. As you read about some of Camille's most difficult cases, you will appreciate how her application of sound clinical judgment often prevented adverse patient outcomes. Sadly, unlike when we were in school and spent so much time on the same units and really got to know nursing staff, experienced nurses have little time to share their wisdom with novice nurses, or the generational gap is too wide to bridge. In *Duty Shoes*, Camille shares many "pearls of wisdom" and new graduates will find much expert advice to help sharpen clinical decision-making skills they may have missed while in their nursing program.

During our orientation to nursing school, Camille wrote that her reason for wanting to be a nurse was because she wanted to "help people." With a few exceptions, that's the reason the majority of nurses endure the physical and mental pain of caring for our patients. Although nursing salaries have certainly increased since my first RN paycheck of $4.10 per hour, no amount of money can adequately compensate direct care nurses. We care for patients and their loved ones at some of the worst moments of their lives, but we also are privileged to share in many intimate and joyous events. As you read this book, you will share in many of those best and worst moments Camille experienced over the years. Tissues may come in handy when you read some of the passages. A nurse must love the profession to continue working for the nearly forty years as Camille has. Read this book and you will quickly realize her love for nursing and her patients. But you will also be touched by the love her patients showed her when they saw her later in the grocery store or at church. Perhaps it is her description of the richness of life in a small town where everyone knows one another that helps the love shine through. Anyone hesitant to move to a small town or rural area to work in health care should read this memoir to gain a greater appreciation for the quality of life outside the "city".

Nursing programs affiliated with large health science centers cannot adequately prepare a nurse for the realities of working in a small hospital. When I taught advanced trauma nursing in the late 1980s, I often heard nurses refer to our major university medical center as "mecca". When I was a clinical nurse, I worked in small, rural hospitals and large medical centers. I understand the reality of being the only RN on a unit or at a code. Camille and other nurses working in these small outlying hospitals deserve tremendous praise for their dedication and the quality of care they deliver in some of the most difficult circumstances. The easy, narrative "story-telling" in this book brings to life so many of the nursing specialty areas such as obstetrics, home health, emergency care, pediatrics and general medical-surgical duty. And, in these small town or rural hospitals, nurses have to be extremely knowledgeable yet able to adapt and transition from one specialty to another, depending on the immediate need of patients on their unit. Nursing students can benefit from the vivid descriptions of homes Camille visited, her harrowing rides in the back of ambulances and the detailed descriptions of nursing care delivery.

Duty Shoes brings so many of Camille's memories to life and can also remind nurses of our generation of the many changes in nursing and healthcare over the past forty years. As a nurse educator, I have occasionally remarked to students about some of the "firsts" I saw over the years: identification of HIV/AIDS, our pharmacy staff preparing chemotherapy rather than the nurses in the med room, using computers on the nursing unit, and family members being allowed to visit at will rather than during strict visiting hours. As I'm recounting some of those memories, students often look at me as if I have two horns growing from my head. Our generation of nurses witnessed many remarkable discoveries in technology, pharmaceuticals, prevention and care delivery. The easy read through this book will remind us of ways these advances have improved patient care and our duties, but also the importance of why we entered the profession. I am pleased to have shared in a few of these memories Camille detailed in her book and proud of the dedication she and others from our program have shown over the decades since graduation.

If you're a seasoned nurse and your passion for nursing has begun to wane, I hope reading Camille's account of her experiences will reignite your love for nursing and you will become an advocate for our profession and help preserve our rich traditions. To those nurses with twenty or thirty years in this profession, my desire is that after reading how Camille retooled and transitioned between specialties, you will dispense with any thoughts of retirement. Find a new passion, perhaps in another nursing specialty area; remember, it is never too late to acquire new skills and knowledge. For those of you just beginning your nursing journey, my hope is that you can look back forty years from now and recount similar stories of your patients and the gratitude they expressed for your love and care. Finally, I hope you each enjoy reading this memoir as much as I have.

Jennan Atkins Phillips, PhD, MSN, RN
Assistant Professor and Director,
NIOSH Deep South Education and Research Center Occupational Health Nursing Graduate Programs
Scholar, PAHO/WHO Collaborating Center for International Nursing
University of Alabama at Birmingham, Birmingham, AL

Preface

Like many little girls growing up in the early sixties, Santa Claus left a doctor's kit for me one Christmas. It was a white plastic case with a red cross on it. Inside was a stethoscope, a thermometer, a pair of red glasses, and a "shot giver." I loved my doctor's kit and played with it for hours on our front porch doctoring on all my baby dolls. I can remember my grandmother visiting one summer when I was about ten years old. Every day she watched *General Hospital* starring Jessie Brewer, RN. I thought Jessie Brewer was the neatest person ever. She always wore her white uniform and her nurse's cap with a black stripe. I wanted to be a nurse just like her.

My career decision was sealed when I was thirteen. I visited my mother when she had her gallbladder removed at a big city hospital. I was completely taken with the huge building, the nurses, the nuns, and all that my mother endured with her operation. Yes, I had decided that I wanted to be a nurse when I grew up. My plans of a nursing career were further encouraged by joining The Future Nurses Club in high school. I attended monthly meetings during school hours. Sometimes a nurse or other medical professional came to speak to us. We did volunteer work at our local hospital to give us a taste of what it was like to be inside a hospital. We observed some of the duties of nurses and filled water pitchers for patients.

I began my nursing journey in the fall of 1973. WOW! Forty years ago! Since that time, I've performed hands-on nursing in several capacities and continue to this day working as a staff RN in a busy labor and delivery unit. What a great experience. There is no career more rewarding than nursing. It hasn't been the "Jessie Brewer" limelight nursing career, but a career of hard work, memorable experiences—both happy and sad—with the satisfaction of knowing that you made a difference in someone's life.

I invite you to come with me on my nursing journey. Put on your "duty shoes" so you can keep up. I want you to experience the things I've done. I want you to see what I've seen, touch what I've touched, and feel emotions that I've felt. Older nurses, I hope you enjoy reliving the "old days" and remembering how it used to be. For nurses who are currently practicing, I hope you appreciate the changes made over the years for the better. For those of you who have just begun nursing, or even thinking about it, I hope you experience the excitement and rewards that a nursing career can give.

Table of Contents

Chapter One 1

Chapter Two 10

Chapter Three 18

Chapter Four...27

Chapter Five 35

Chapter Six 40

Chapter Seven...53

Chapter Eight..70

Chapter Nine...84

Chapter Ten...104

Chapter Eleven 117

Chapter Twelve 125

Chapter Thirteen...152

Chapter Fourteen 155

Chapter Fifteen..168

Chapter Sixteen...171

Chapter Seventeen 185

Common Terms Then and Now 191

Chapter One

NURSING SCHOOL FIRST YEAR
1973–1974

One-by-one we arrived at the school of nursing for freshman orientation the Tuesday after Labor Day in 1973. Students came from all over Central Alabama to begin their nursing journey at the hospital-based diploma program. Also known as a three-year program, these nursing schools are the oldest and offer the most traditional type of education receiving much of the training in the hospital. Diploma graduates take the same state board exams as BSN and ASN graduates and are issued the same licensure.

We gathered in the large classroom quietly awaiting instructions. Most of our class consisted of young females right out of high school, but some were women who were married with children. In the middle of the room amongst all of us females was a "token male." wearing a white uniform. *Who was this bald man? Is there such a thing as a male nurse?* He probably felt as if everybody was looking at him. Well, they were.

The school's director came in and gave the customary orientation. Each one of us was given a piece of paper with instructions to write an essay as to why we wanted to become a nurse. Mine was short and to the point. I wanted to be a nurse so that I could help people. She gathered our essays and we were dismissed.

After lunch we moved into our dorm rooms. By the end of the

day faces became familiar and names easier to remember. That evening the school hosted a picnic as a "Meet and Greet" for faculty and students. Each of us stood, introduced ourselves and told where we were from. I discovered that the male student was from my hometown and my daddy was his teacher in high school. The school of nursing was not only affiliated with the hospital adjacent to it, but also a junior college in another town.

We were eager to get started and immediately jumped into the school's curriculum. Our first quarter began with the Philosophy of Nursing taught by the director of the school. The same instructor taught us Fundamentals of Nursing I and II. She made learning fun. One of the most important things she taught us was that "if you tell a patient that you will do something always keep your word."

The first thing we learned was how to wash our hands correctly using proper technique—by turning the water off with a paper towel, not our clean bare hands. Next, we learned how to work the manual bed. It had a handle underneath that cranked the bed to change positions and a lever to raise the knees called a knee-gatch. She instructed us how to give baths, take temperatures, pulse and respirations (TPRs,) blood pressures and change bed linens. Temperatures were taken with mercury thermometers either under the arm, under the tongue, or rectally. We were shown how to wrap bath cloths around our hands making a bath mitten. Bed-making was an art, complete with mitered corners, draw-sheet, fan-folded sheets and toe pleat. The draw-sheet helped to protect the bottom sheet and was used to help turn patients. I learned to change pillow cases without using my chin. These things are known as A.M. care.

Our manikin was named Madam Chase. We practiced giving her baths and as well as to our fellow students. Along with the baths we learned range of motion exercises and the prevention of bed sores. Classmates checked one another's vital signs.

After we "passed off" these skills we began patient care in the nursing home which was connected to the hospital. There, our instructors "passed off" the skill while we performed them on patients. It was weird bathing people, but that was part of it. We encouraged the patients to do their own mouth care, but usually we brushed their false teeth for them. We were mindful of their false teeth when taking up meal trays being careful not to send them away with the trays. If you let that happen you would have to retrieve them. At this point, we had not received our uniforms so we wore white lab coats. We did lose a couple of students during our nursing home stint. I think the school started us there to weed out those who wouldn't make it.

Our instructors taught us about professional appearance and how to take care of ourselves. It was strongly encouraged that we wear support hose, get plenty of rest, and eat right. We were so excited when our uniforms, or "U-Nees," arrived. We tried them on making sure they fit. The length of the uniform was very important—just below the knee. They were traditional student uniforms, light blue with white aprons and skirts. We were told not to wear them around town, only in clinicals. Our solid white caps indicated we were freshmen. We could not wear our caps while driving to or from clinicals. I still have my small white name tag with blue writing, "Miss Foshee Nursing Student." My first pair of duty shoes was Clinics and cost eighteen dollars. We were told to polish our shoes with Sani White shoe polish. I was kind of lax on the shoes. I hated polishing them. Some of the girls shined and buffed their shoes every night. Not me, maybe once a month. I easily snagged a run in my white hose, having to constantly buy new ones. We wore no jewelry except a wrist watch with a second hand. The married students could wear their wedding bands. Our hair was up off our collars. No polished fingernails or perfume was allowed. We never chewed gum in clinicals.

Shortly after our arrival, we began our college courses thirty miles away. We rode a school bus with the oldest member of our class being the driver. Our classes included anatomy, physiology, chemistry, microbiology, psychology, sociology, nutrition, and English. It was kind of embarrassing when the long yellow bus pulled up at the junior college parking lot while the other students looked on, sometimes shouting, "Here come the nurses!"

By December we were doing clinicals at the hospital, mostly on the medical floor, the fourth floor. Every afternoon before next day clinicals, we went to the hospital, met our patients, and reviewed the patient's chart. We continued to "pass off" required skills transitioning them into the hospital setting. Some of the floors had four bed wards. There were female wards and male wards. The wards and semi-private rooms did have curtains, so we attempted to maintain the patient's privacy during toileting and baths.

Bedpans were made of stainless steel, so they were reusable, heavy, and noisy. We toted many bedpans and potty buckets—covered with a towel—down the hall to the hopper room to empty them. The towel hid the contents, but not the smell. I'd never seen a hopper before. It was pretty intimidating and looked like a huge square commode that could suck you in if you got too close. We cleaned the bedpans in the hopper room and sent them downstairs to be sanitized. After being sanitized they were sent up in paper sleeves and stored for use. At the end of each shift the mercury thermometers were gathered from the patient rooms and sent down for cleaning. A clean batch was sent up at the beginning of each shift. Other patient items such as emesis basins, water pitchers, bath basins, urinals, and suction bottles were also reusable.

∂∘⟨

We began our second quarter with Fundamentals of Nursing II, broadening our observation and assessment skills. This quarter we learned how to do urinary catheterizations, hypodermic injections, sterile dressing changes, and enemas. We practiced drawing up sterile water and injecting it into oranges over and over again. We carried oranges, water, needles, and syringes around for days practicing to get the skill just right.

Then came the day we were required to give a shot to one another in front of the class and the instructors. We paired up. When I stuck the needle into my partner, she jumped pulling the needle out. I had to stick her again. After perfecting our skills, we took them to the Medical-Surgical floors.

The second floor, or surgical floor, was new to us as we began clinicals with preoperative and postoperative patients. Some of the patients required a shave prep and some required enemas prior to surgery. We administered the IM (intramuscular) pre-op medications. When the patients returned from surgery we cared for them becoming familiar with routine care and surgeons orders. We finally got to change dressings on a real patient utilizing sterile technique. The most difficult part was getting the sterile gloves on correctly being careful not to contaminate them.

One of my most unforgettable surgery patients was a young woman who had under gone a radical mastectomy who had an impressive incision. The surgery involved removing her breast and the underlying muscles giving the appearance that the chest was sunken. The long incision began near her clavicle and extended vertically the length of her ribcage. There was a Hemovac in place that gently suctioned blood and secretions from the wound that we measured, emptied, recharged, and documented the amount at the end of each shift. She kept a picture of her little girl at her bedside.

Post-op pain medications were given intramuscularly. We mixed some of the pain medications ourselves using sterile water and tablets in a vial. I recall morphine was one of those meds and it was ordered in grains.

We became acquainted with medical equipment such as oxygen and suction machines. Oxygen was kept in a tank or cylinder at the bedside. There were oxygen masks, but most of the patients used oxygen tents for therapy. We learned how to set them up and maintain them, since there were no respiratory therapists. The sheets were tucked in a certain way to keep the oxygen inside the tent. We were mindful of any kind of open flame around any oxygen.

Another piece of equipment was the Gumco or "roll-around suction" machine. With this we learned how to suction patients and how to manage NG (nasogastric) tubes to suction. We measured, emptied, and rinsed the glass bottle of the Gumco at the end of every shift. Stomach contents can be very vile. Sometimes I would gag when emptying them.

Pharmacology of Nursing was taught in the third quarter. With this, it was a *must* to pass the dreaded "Dosages and Solutions" test in order to continue in school. We had to figure dosages using formulas, without a calculator. I'd always struggled in math, but I studied hard for that test and passed it.

Giving medications was a big step; there was no room for error. You could kill a patient with the wrong medicine. Clear and cloudy had a new meaning as we learned to mix and administer insulin. Pills and solutions were kept in the medicine room and were dispensed from a multi-dose pill bottle or vial. We took the oral medications to the bedside in small paper cups.

I recall one of the students gave a patient Betadine-a topical solution-by mouth. Word got around quickly if you made a mistake. We used disposable syringes and needles. We carefully recapped the needles, broke them from the syringe, and threw them in the trash. A glass canister held alcohol soaked cotton balls used to clean the skin before administering injections.

A typical day for the freshman dorm student began at 6 AM. My roommate and I jumped out of bed at the sound of the wind-up alarm clock. We dressed and were walking into the hospital cafeteria by 6:30 AM. The best meal of the day was breakfast which we ate quickly. By 6:45 we were *standing* around the desk at our assigned nurse's station awaiting the nurses shift report. We never sat at the nurse's desk. The nurses at the desk always stood when a doctor was present. We gave A.M. care, meds, and treatments until 10 AM, three days a week. We reported off and returned to the cafeteria for an early lunch. By 10:45 we'd eaten lunch, changed clothes and were boarding the bus to the junior college. We returned around 4:30 in the afternoon and went back to the cafeteria for supper. The food was pretty good, but I'm not picky. We got a good meal for less than a dollar. The other two weekdays were either spent in nursing classes or clinicals.

Since the classroom and the library were connected to student housing, dorm students had an advantage over the commuters. We could use them anytime even after hours. We did hours of research in the library using reference materials especially the *American Journal of Nursing*, or AJNs. We scoured over tons of articles using the information in our research papers that we wrote in longhand or sometimes typed. When we needed a break from studying we went over to the 'P' section and pulled out a *Playgirl*. That really got our minds off nursing.

June was a busy month for the whole school. The seniors were working their night shift rotation so we were considerate of them sleeping in the dorm during the daytime. Graduation was coming up and the first and second year students had to sing as part of the graduation program. The seniors graduated and the second year students left for summer break. We began the summer quarter doing clinicals in the hospital in Medical-Surgical nursing. We began our first medical-surgical class with GU, or genitourinary system. Our instructor was a great teacher who taught us Med-Surg until we graduated.

At this point we were working in the hospital every day, either eight hours or part of the shift. I could tell the LPNs and nurses' aides loved having us there since we did most of the A.M. care, meds and treatments. Much of our time was spent emptying bedpans, potty chairs, urinals, Foley catheters, and Gumcos. We perfected enemas that summer. The 3-H enema, "high, hot, and hell of a lot," became a household word. By the end of that summer, we became very efficient and could really turn out the work. Bathing patients, even men, had become an everyday thing.

Patient beds were changed every day, putting the top sheet on the bottom if unsoiled. There were no fitted sheets. We placed the dirty linen in the pillow case and carried it to the soiled linen room.

Our instructors were close by, especially in the medicine room. We charted on the I&O (intake and output) sheets, graphic sheets (vital sign charting), and nurses notes. After each shift we discussed our day with our instructors. They taught us "if you don't chart it, then you didn't do it."

In my first year I had my most memorable patient, a young woman with a brain tumor called a Glioblastoma, an extremely aggressive form of cancer. Her husband cared for her at home for as long as he could. She became unresponsive requiring total care. Medicines were given IM or through her NG tube. She required bed baths, Foley care, suctioning, and NG feedings. The liquid diet of pureed food was poured into a 60cc syringe and administered by gravity flow. She was my patient for many shifts until she died.

This first year was so important to our training. It was the foundation that supported the next two years. Our instructors guided us through our skills, giving us confidence and teaching us how not only to care for, but how to interact with patients. By the end of the first year, I knew I had made the right career choice. I loved nursing. It became a part of me and I became a part of it.

MISS FOSHEE
NURSING STUDENT

Med-Surg Class

Med-Surg Instructor

Chapter Two

NURSING SCHOOL SECOND YEAR 1974–1975

In September of '74 we began our second year of training. All of our junior college courses were completed so it was all nursing for the remaining two years. This year we picked up a few more students. Some came from a nursing school up north that closed. We wore a single black strip on the corner of our caps, signifying we were second year students. My second year I applied and received a state nursing scholarship for six hundred dollars. The only requirement was to work in the state of Alabama for a year. We lived in the dorm free and the cafeteria meals were cheap. The scholarship paid for most everything including tuition. My parents gave me a little money for gas and to occasionally eat out. Gas was only fifty cents a gallon, so twenty-five dollars went a long way. With my extra money I made working as a nurse's aide, I had everything I needed.

Our class was divided into three groups for specialized nursing courses: Psychiatrics, Obstetrics, and Pediatrics. Along with care plans and med cards, we began doing case studies on patients. There were eleven of us in our "Psych" rotation that traveled to the private psychiatric hospital an hour away three days a week. Seven of us, including the driver piled into the hospital station wagon at 6:30 AM for the drive to the big city. When we got there we received our assignments. We visited our patients, wrote interpersonal relationship or IPR notes, and turned them in to our instructor. Sometimes we *ad libbed* on the notes. I was sick of writing IPR notes by the end of the three months. But it was still interesting to learn about different psychiatric conditions in class and then interact with patients having those conditions.

On occasion our instructor accompanied us into the "locked-down unit" which isolated certain patients from the rest of the population. I had an uneasy feeling when the heavy door slammed and I was locked in that part of the facility. You never knew what you'd see there. Seeing some of these patients was upsetting to say the least. I witnessed patients in straight-jackets crying, screaming, and rocking back and forth. Their room contained only a bed.

There were many young patients there with alcohol and drug problems. I recall an older lady that lived in the hospital. I suppose she had a lot of money to be able to stay there. On the walls of her room were pictures of a young woman torn from magazines. She told us that the model was her daughter which we learned was untrue.

We observed patients undergo electroconvulsive therapy, also known as "shock treatments." This was done early in the mornings with the patients NPO (nothing by mouth). Electrodes were attached to their head and an electronic current was given causing a grand mal seizure. The patient usually slept after the procedure. It was quite impressive and I didn't like watching it. The patients were given several in a series to obtain the desired response in the treatment of depression.

We did interact with patients there, but we also spent much of our time in the recreation room. I learned to play foosball and got pretty good at it. We all became addicted to the new soap opera, *The Young and the Restless,* that quarter.

As part of our psychiatric training, we visited the crisis center listening to conversations of the call-ins and how the trained workers handled the calls. We observed individuals in half-way houses who were transitioning from psychiatric facilities into the community. Locally, we visited psychiatric patients in their homes through the county mental health office. We did not make these visits alone, but were paired with another student. Our patient was a middle-aged man that we always found sitting on his porch wearing overalls. He was a patient at a psychiatric hospital and returned to his home. He didn't talk much, but answered questions when asked. He was friendly and we never felt threatened there.

Growing up in Alabama I'd heard of the "Insane Asylum," Bryce Hospital. I never thought I would visit there. We drove to Tuscaloosa and spent the day at Bryce Hospital, a hospital for the mentally ill and Partlow, an institution for the mentally disabled. Partlow was the most depressing place I've ever been. It was sad to see patients my age—nineteen—lying in baby beds being fed with bottles. Others walked around wearing helmets for protection. There were so many patients at Bryce. It was unbelievable.

I left Tuscaloosa feeling sad and depressed, but gained a renewed appreciation and thankfulness for my life. Psych nursing was interesting, but three months was enough for me.

A few months after our psych rotation, *One Flew Over the Cuckoo's Nest*, was released in theaters. We made a special trip to the city to see it.

༺ঙৎ༻

Pediatrics was a long three months. Our Peds instructor was a very smart woman, but sometimes I had a hard time grasping what she said when she explained things. We began in the classroom then hit the pediatric unit eager to nurse children. It was hard to get vital signs on a wiggling toddler. The thermometer had to be held in place for three minutes. Sometimes I could get it easier if they were sleeping, but slipping the thermometer under their arm was a skill in itself.

I remember dehydrated babies and toddlers sometimes had hypodermoclysis, or clysis, the administration of fluids subcutaneously. It was usually done with two needles placed in the thighs. It looked so painful in their little legs; I couldn't ever imagine placing one. We poured sugary liquids down them, gave injections in their thighs an inserted suppositories in their rectums.

No wonder they cried when we entered their room.

My most memorable peds patient was a one month old baby girl with whooping cough. I could never hold and rock her because she had to stay in one of the clear isolettes. She was my patient several shifts. I kept her clean and tried to feed her. You can't imagine how much she coughed. I rubbed her skin and talked to her. One morning I came to the floor for my shift, assuming I would take care of her that day and she was gone. She died during the night. Still makes me sad to think about her.

Another patient I remember was a toddler who was recovering from meningitis. His mama had set him in a high chair and he was feeding himself breakfast. I was in the room making his bed and noticed him struggling to breathe. He choked on the eggs and was turning blue unable to get his breath. His mama started screaming and crying. I jerked him out of the high chair, tuned him head down and popped him between his shoulder blades with the palm of my hand. He threw up all in the floor and on my shoes. He began to cry, so I knew he was all right. If they can cry, they can breathe.

Our pediatric rotation group traveled to the state's school for children who were deaf and blind; another "eye opener" making me appreciate my life. It was amazing what these kids could do. I remember a woman at the school for the deaf playing cords on a black grand piano. The children put their hands on the piano and signed if the cords were little or big by feeling the vibration. Amazing.

As part of our pediatric training we worked in the pediatrician's office across from the hospital doing assessments, assisting the doctors, and administering hypodermics to children. I could do *some* peds nursing, but I couldn't see myself practicing in peds exclusively.

కొ∞ఆ

Obstetrics or Maternal Child Health was one of the most exciting three months of nursing school. Most of our small group enjoyed doing clinicals on the OB/GYN floor, the third floor. We were divided into three smaller groups for four weeks of labor and delivery, four weeks of postpartum and four weeks of nursery. We began the course in the classroom with our instructor who was very prim and proper. She had never had children, but knew everything about birthing babies and the care of newborns. She illustrated the labor and delivery process with a baby doll in a crocheted uterus. She got the point across. We practiced gowning and gloving using sterile technique in the classroom and took that into the delivery room where we set up the delivery table, draped and prepped the patients. We became familiar with the OB instruments and what each one was used for. We changed into white scrub dresses to work in any OB department.

There were two obstetricians and maybe a general practitioner that delivered babies. Occasionally, a nurse would catch one when the doctor didn't get there in time. Unless a laboring patient was about to deliver, we gave them a soap suds enema and a perineal shave upon admission. Caring for women in labor was a reality-check. Some of the labor patients cried softly and some bellowed out blood-curdling screams. They were given Demerol, a narcotic, and Largon, a sedative, IM for pain. When they progressed to eight "sonameters" we sat them up and the obstetrician administered a saddle block, a type of spinal anesthesia that gives pain relief to the saddle area of a patient helping them get through the rest of labor and the delivery.

Most of the deliveries were performed with forceps. The obstetrician used green soap to lubricate the forceps before sliding them inside the mother around the baby's head, another impressive sight.

After the baby was born, it was handed to the nurse or the student. Forceps' marks on the newborn were a common thing. Once the mother was cleaned up, we gave her a Deladumone injection IM to suppress the production of milk. Few mothers breast fed back then. We perfected our IM injection skills during our labor and delivery rotation. The mothers with saddle blocks had to remain flat for twelve hours to prevent a spinal headache. We soon felt comfortable in L&D.

We cared for the mothers on the post-partum units, taking vital signs, doing fundal checks, giving peri-care consisting of sitz baths and using peri-lights. Perilghts were light bulbs mounted in a square wooden box. I saw some bad looking bottoms; swollen and discolored, assuming this was the norm for those who just delivered. We scrubbed the community bath tubs after each use so it would be clean for the next patient.

One day I was assisting a student in catheterizing one of the delivered patients. We positioned the patient and as the student was prepping the perineal area with a betadine soaked cotton ball, two marble-sized blue balls fell out. *What were those?*

We gasped and looked at each other trying to keep straight faces until the procedure was finished. Our instructor explained that the patient had some varicosities that prolapsed from the vagina.

We administered preoperative and post-operative care for Cesarean section and GYN patients. We changed dressings daily using sterile technique. The surgery patients were not allowed to get their incisions wet, so no showering until the "stitches were removed." Patients and their husbands were always asking how many stitches there were, whether from a C-section or a perineal repair. *Who counts stitches?*

The newborn nursery was a huge room with small cribs and rocking chairs. The screened windows were open this time of year. We were responsible for newborn care, baths, feedings, TPRs and cord care. I was shocked to see that some of the babies had long heads. My friend and I called them "cucumber heads" but soon learned it was only molding and would resolve in a few days. One of the students painted not only the base of the baby's cord with gentian violet antiseptic, but painted the whole abdomen. Our instructor was so mad.

During our OB training we were assigned a patient that we followed for three months as a case-study. We met her at the clinic for her OB appointments. We followed her through her labor, delivery and post-partum period. Our case-study was turned in at the end of the quarter. We also worked in the GYN clinic assisting with pap smears and examinations.

I loved obstetrics; I could see myself being an OB nurse one day.

By the end of the second year, we knew and had worked under most of the head nurses in each unit. I was in awe of them. I hoped I could be as good as they were one day. Not only did they look professional, but were so confident and knowledgeable.

We continued to build on the foundations of our first year expanding our knowledge and skills. We constantly learned about different diseases, medicines, and treatments, as we evolved into nurses.

As busy as we were, we still found time for some extracurricular activities with classmates. Our director invited and encouraged us to attend the student nurse's state convention in Birmingham, Alabama in March of '75. Many of us went and stayed at the Parliament House. There we met other nursing students from all over the state and enjoyed comparing notes about their schools.

After twenty-one months of classes and hospital clinicals we'd earned and were given a summer break. Most of us went back to our hometown to work as nurse's aides or LPNs. When we returned we would be in the home-stretch.

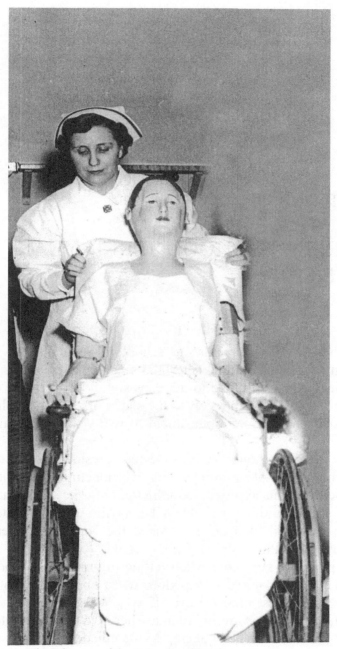

The Director of the School and Madame Chase

Chapter Three

NURSING SCHOOL THIRD YEAR 1975–1976

I was excited to return to school in September to reconnect with my classmates and enter the final year of nursing school. Another stripe was added to our caps signifying we were third-year student nurses. I again received the state nurse's scholarship for the year increasing my reimbursement to two years. What an exciting year.

It was an honor being elected president of the Student Government Association presiding over meetings with the students and being a liaison with administration. The Alabama Student Nurse's convention was held in Huntsville and I attended that in March. In April, two of us attended the National Student Nurses Convention in Philadelphia, Pennsylvania.

I played it very cool when telling my mama and daddy good-bye in the terminal, but was anxious when I boarded the huge plane. This was the first time I'd ever flown. We grabbed window seats and in no time we were in Atlanta where we changed onto an even bigger plane. I remember seeing Mohammed Ali and his entourage as we walked through the Atlanta Airport.

We attended the meetings and did some sight-seeing while there. To add to our excitement, the song "Philadelphia Freedom" was heard frequently on the radio while we were there. It was as if Elton John had written that song for us.

As third year students we traveled to Auburn University to help with the Red Cross blood drive. We took vital signs, did finger sticks and assisted the donors with paper work.

I recall sitting at the table when a big fellow that had just donated came over and sat down beside me. As I passed him a plate of cookies he fell over on me. We lowered him to the floor and gave him a whiff of ammonia that brought him around. How embarrassing for the poor guy. Guess he was a little dehydrated.

Our third year focused on medical surgical nursing. We studied the disorders by systems: cardiovascular, respiratory, gastrointestinal, musculoskeletal and neurological. It seemed like when we studied a specific illness, that some of us would have the symptom. For instance, I had twinges in my right side when we learned about appendicitis. After class we compared our symptoms laughing about them.

We worked on the medical and surgical floors. We perfected the sterile dressing changes and the removal of sutures. Sutures were removed one-by-one, by holding the knot with a hemostat, cutting below the knot and pulling the stitch through. We assumed nursing care of not only general surgery patients, but of post-op vascular and orthopedic patients.

The class was divided into small groups for our surgery rotation. We were very excited to see an operation and to eventually scrub with the surgeon. We practiced in the class room for hours perfecting sterile technique with gowning and gloving. We learned the instruments by name and passed them to each other trying to make a "popping" sound as it hit our gloved hand. My mind was inundated with images of surgical instruments, seeing them when I closed my eyes at night.

After hours of preparation, the day finally came that we were to observe in the operating room. We changed into the gray scrub dresses and hats. We were excited. The first case for observation was a vasectomy. Whoops. It was a student's father so we had to move to the next operating room which was a hemorrhoidectomy. We were instructed by our instructor and the operating room nurses, "DO NOT TOUCH ANYTHING!"

We entered the room single file, lining the walls, and keeping our hands close to our bodies standing like statues. Upon entering the operating room, the first thing I saw was the patient's butt up in the air and all exposed. Yes, he was mooning us and he didn't even know it. He was anesthetized and placed in the "jack knife" position.

We observed the surgeon, the nurses, and the nurse anesthetist. There was no anesthesiologist. The sterile drapes were reusable. They were gathered, washed, folded, packaged, and sterilized by the OR nurses. There were no surgical techs, only an orderly that cleaned the rooms after each case.

This team of OR nurses ran four rooms. The major cases were done in OR One and OR Two. OR Three was the cysto room and the fourth room was for minor cases. In the cysto room, cystoscopies were done to examine the urethra and bladder with a cystoscope utilizing a special light with the ability of taking biopsies if needed and a room for minor surgeries. After watching a few cases, we became comfortable and began helping the nurses. Some of the cases were very long and tedious. I don't know how the nurses stood so long holding retractors. I remember one of the surgeons doing a thyroidectomy that took six hours.

After passing the OR skills test in the classroom we had to scrub a case with one of the surgeons. One of my classmates passed out while scrubbed in and fell on the Mayo stand, which is a portable instrument stand that is positioned over the patient during surgery.

My big day had arrived. It was my turn to scrub in and honestly I was scared to death. In preparation, I scrubbed finger tips to the elbow with Phisohex for three minutes on each hand using a brush and orange sticks. Nervously, I entered the operating room where I gowned and gloved. I meticulously set up the instruments on the Mayo stand while my instructor watched every move I made. Carefully, I climbed onto the stool taking my position beside the tall surgeon.

He was not only a good doctor, but a good teacher, taking time to explain things to me. I flinched as he made the initial cut on the abdomen. It reminded me of fingernails scraping on a chalkboard, without the noise. I handed the instruments as he called for them attempting to make them pop in his glove.

Once he was in the abdomen, he said to me," lay your hand in mine and I will guide it around inside her abdomen."

I wasn't expecting that, but I did get to feel some of her organs. He removed her gall bladder and laid it on the mayo stand in front of me. It was a blue-green color. I stayed focused and upright the entire case. When the case was completed, the surgeon took a scalpel and opened the gallbladder so I could see what was inside. He pointed out the small stones covered in slimy bile.

As part of our surgery rotation, we worked in the Recovery Room observing and assessing patients immediately after surgery. There were no monitors. We took the patients vital signs manually and documented them on the graph sheet and wrote notes in the nurses' notes. Upon awakening, the patients were sick, throwing up, and in severe pain. If the patient was a child it was ten times worse, screaming and crying. Many had to be held down on the gurney. The recovery room nurse never left the bedside of a recovering patient.

The operating room was a fascinating place, but not a place I wanted to work in. Once was enough for me to feel around in someone's abdomen.

We did a six week rotation in the intensive care unit taking care of some of the sickest medical and surgical patients. In the ICU we learned to care for the immediate post-op patients of vascular and thoracic surgeries. Many of the patients had long incisions and were connected to various tubes. There, I learned trach (tracheostomy) skills. I recall the first IV I started. It was with a large bore needle with success on the first try. I wrapped the arm on a long arm board with layers of rolled gauze. We practiced starting IVs in the classroom lab on Madam Chase and each other. We did not wear gloves for venipunctures or injections.

Two students were paired for the Emergency Room (ER) rotation. With such a large class it took a while for everyone to rotate through.

The ER held many amazing experiences. Included in our ER rotation we observed one of the nurse anesthetists hypnotize a couple of patients to change their permanent trachs. The patients focused on a pocket watch she swung back and forth. It was incredible.

One Friday, a young man brought his wife into the ER with a headache. She was brushing her teeth when the headache began. It evolved into excruciating pain and soon she began having seizures. My classmate and I assisted the nurses and doctor with a spinal tap where they found high pressure and bloody spinal fluid. She had some sort of brain hemorrhage. The decision was made to transfer her to Birmingham to University Hospital and we were asked to go with her. Eagerly we accepted the request for our first ambulance ride. With a blood pressure cuff, a stethoscope, a padded tongue blade, and a syringe of Valium we climbed into the ambulance with the unresponsive patient. We were instructed to "keep her on her side." She had no IV line so the Valium was given IM in route.

We positioned ourselves at her head and her side. Her pitiful husband sat at the foot of the stretcher sobbing all the way to Birmingham. She was a critical transfer so the sirens and lights were turned on as soon as we left the parking lot. Once getting on the main highway, the driver "gunned it." That's when we buckled up and held on. The normal fifty minute ride took thirty minutes. State troopers blocked the incoming roads at the intersections to avoid the ambulance having to stop.

When we got to the city, the ambulance driver drove around cars and up on the medians. My friend and I were scared to death. Never had we ever experienced anything like that. We got there safely and the attendants quickly rushed her into the ER. She had several seizures in route. Unfortunately, the cerebral hemorrhage took her life.

After our rotation in the ER, my friend said she thought she had found her niche. She's been in the ER most of her nursing career.

By May we had completed the thick Med-Surg book. We felt well prepared to go out into the nurse work force and function as new graduates. We mastered the skills and had done everything Registered Nurses do with the exception of transfusing blood.

As part of the curriculum, we worked as preceptors choosing the unit. Most of us applied for and had job offers before graduating. The last two weeks of clinicals were done on the night shift on the medical-surgical floors working as the head nurse of the floor. We became certified in CPR; a two-day class taught by two of our instructors with manikins borrowed from the American Heart Association.

Our final nursing class was Leadership and Management taught by the director of the school. She was very dedicated to our profession. I believe that she provided some students a chance at a nursing career that otherwise couldn't have been attained. During our three years she kept a very close watch on each of us. If anyone stepped out of line or their grades were not to her liking, she called the student to her office for a conference. She kept our essays that we wrote on the first day of school on why we wanted to become nurses returning them to us on the last day of class.

During my three years at the hospital I noticed the RNs wearing wool navy capes with a red lining during the winter months. I wanted one so bad! The initials of our school were embroidered on the collar. We were offered a chance to order one. I saved up thirty dollars and bought one. I was so proud of that cape. I still have it.

Our class was very close, always being together and relying on one another for three years. There was another constant in our training, the instructors. Some of them were clinical instructors, others were classroom instructors and some were in both roles. The school added instructors, but I don't recall any of them leaving while we were there. The Psyche teacher retired the year we graduated. Most of the instructors were graduates of our school. We always respected them whether we were in the classroom, in clinicals, or at a school event such as a picnic or the annual spring formal.

☞◦☜

It was a Friday afternoon before graduation when I was driving home. The windows of my '73 Camaro were down, the eight-track rocking and rolling, not a care in the world. I topped a hill and saw cars stopped below. I slowly pulled up behind them wondering what had happened. I got out of my car and walked up to the people standing around. Then I saw him, a toddler lying on the side of the road wearing only a diaper. He was pale, lifeless, but had no noticeable wounds. His daddy was bent over him crying. *This was awful. What should I do?*

I went over to him, knelt beside him, and began the steps of CPR that I had recently learned. We were taught to continue until you could no longer physically do it or until the ambulance arrived. I thought the ambulance would never get there. They took him away. He had been hit by a car while playing too close to the road with his brothers and sisters. How things can change in an instant. It was a very sobering weekend.

இ∽இ

The week of graduation was busy with ceremony preparations and moving out of the dorm. One of the doctors hosted a party at his farm for the graduates and the instructors. I remember catching a string of catfish that I could hardly pick up. We played games and some of the students rode horses. One of the graduates fell off a horse and broke her back. The ambulance came and got her. She stayed in the hospital several weeks missing our group picture on the steps of the school, but was allowed to go to graduation and receive her diploma and then return to the hospital.

A couple of days before graduation, I was driving home and passed by the football field when I noticed a boy on a go cart riding in the road. I thought to myself, "He's gonna get hit by a car if he's not careful." Later I rode back through and noticed a blue pickup truck stopped next to the empty go cart. I knew something was wrong; this couldn't be happening again. The boy was lying on the side of the road, pale, but breathing. He had been hit by the pickup truck.

The ambulance came immediately after I arrived. I helped the attendant put him on a stretcher and load him in the ambulance. Holding the oxygen mask on his face, I talked to him on the way to my hometown hospital. I remember seeing the doctor climb into the back of the ambulance when they transferred the boy to a larger hospital. He was a tough kid and recovered from his chest injuries.

The school hosted a Senior Tea honoring the graduates on the day of graduation. Our graduation exercise had a theme "The Spirit of '76." On June 18th, thirty-seven of us marched down the aisle of The First United Methodist Church and took our places in the front pews. We wore white dress uniforms and a white cap with one solid stripe signifying graduate nurses. Alabama Lieutenant Governor, Jerry Beasley, gave the commencement address. Our fundamentals instructor, dressed as Florence Nightingale, led us in the Nightingale Pledge as we held a small lamp. One by one, we received a Bible, our school pins, and our diplomas. The class recessed to "Sweet, Sweet Spirit" sung by the under classmen. After the reception, we were off to the graduation party held at the home of one of my classmates.

After graduation the school offered a state boards review and most of us returned to study. We gathered once more in Birmingham for the two-day state board exam. We sat four to a table in the huge room with only a No. 2 pencil in hand. The licensure test was in six parts, Pediatrics, Psychiatrics, OB, Surgical, Medical and Pharmacology. If you failed it, you only had one chance to repeat the part that was failed. What a relief to get that over with.

Spirit of '76

Graduating Class of 1976

Graduation with our instructor as Florence Nightingale

Chapter Four

DORM LIFE
1973–1976

Dorm life for college students in the seventies was similar for those in a large university in a big city or small nursing school in a rural mill town. Young men and women left home to further their education, adjusting to new surroundings and making new friends. There probably were few co-ed dorms in Alabama in 1973 and ours was one of them.

Built in 1951, our dormitory was a long, white two-story building. First and second year female students occupied the second floor. The community bathroom was centrally located in the middle of the long hall. At one end was a small kitchen with a porch that opened to the outside. The other end of the hall led to the library and classrooms. All third year female and all the male students lived in suites on the first floor. Our house mother had an office to the left of the entrance into the dorm. She lived in an apartment adjacent to her office. Across from her office was a large parlor that we used for dates, parties, or just hanging out between classes. A wide stairwell joined the two floors as there were no elevators. The dorm was connected to the school of nursing and was located across the back parking lot of the hospital.

Roommates were assigned by the school administration. We didn't know who our roommates were until we moved in. The names were posted on the door to our rooms. My roommate never show up, so I stayed by myself the first night. It was a lonely feeling not knowing a soul in the place. I was a little home sick, but that quickly passed. On the second day, a girl assigned down the hall from me moved in as my roommate. She, too, was from a small town. We had a lot in common and made our small dorm room as home-like as possible with matching bedspreads and curtains purchased at Bargain Town, USA. Our black and white TV complete with rabbit ears was the centerpiece.

The first winter was uncomfortably cold, requiring us to wear layers of clothes. There was a small heater in each room that distributed little heat. I recall us playing card games wrapped in our electric blankets.

Our first summer was exasperating. We were usually soaked with sweat as there was no air conditioning. The window fans worked hard to circulate the hot air. A new heating and cooling system was purchased after that first summer making the next two years much more comfortable.

The second summer we cranked the thermostat down so cold that we slept under our electric blankets. Another luxury that was installed about the same time was cable TV. I learned how to splice into the cable that ran the length of the building allowing more channels on our televisions. Yes, dorm life was more enjoyable after the first year. We remained roommates until she married five months before graduation. I was happy for her, but at the same time I was lonesome. I didn't get another roommate, but kept the same suite-mate the remainder of the year.

Soon after we freshman were settled in, the upper class dorm students gave us a party. It was a "Get Acquainted Party" given in the second floor classroom. Entering the room, the first thing we saw was a manikin with a broken leg sitting in an old wooden wheelchair. The food tables were covered with hospital bed sheets. Chips were served in enamel bedpans and bath basins. The French onion dip was served in emesis basins. Punch flowed from enema bags into antique urinals. They used urinals as pitchers to fill our cups. We knew of some sort of gathering the upper-class had planned, but had no idea what it would entail. We were excited to see the creativity of the décor. This little party was the beginning of many lasting friendships.

I loved living in the dorm. We played and studied together. The upper classman "showed us the ropes." Our classes quickly became friends, however as in most social settings, especially schools, cliques began to form. Over the years, some friendships remained constant, others dropped off. I don't recall a lot of "drama" during those years. There wasn't time for that.

One of the duties assigned to the freshman class was the role of ear-piercer. I volunteered, and the honor was handed down to me. I numbed the willing participant's earlobes with ice, dotted the exact spot with a pen, and then stuck an eighteen gauge—a rather large needle—through the earlobe into a wine bottle cork. I quickly pulled the needle out and pushed the earring stud through the hole. It usually worked out. I also learned to arch eyebrows. Of course, this was done with a pair of tweezers.

Many of us had long hair, the straighter the better. We ironed each other's hair by draping our hair over an ironing board and ironing with the clothes iron being careful not to have the iron too hot. One of the second-year students cut hair. She could cut the perfect shag by pulling the hair up in a ponytail on top of the head, then cutting above the rubber band. It worked beautifully. As a result of this easy to come by style, there were several students with the same haircut.

Smoking was allowed on the premises. I was surprised to see how many students smoked. Alcohol was prohibited, but sometimes we smuggled it into the dorm anyway. We learned some of those tricks from our older and wiser upper classmen. For example, it was fairly easy to sneak in a bottle of wine in some sort of bag. The wine favorite among the nursing students was Boone's Farm. A safe hiding place was a dirty clothes duffle bag. Some of the students hid their vodka in the library under "V." One of the students lowered a rope from the second floor porch as one of the older boyfriends of one of the freshman tied an eight-pack of Miller ponies to a rope and hoisted it up. Most of us were under age, but there were plenty of older students who bought it. The student's favorite convenience store was Yonders Blossom. The upper classmen took us to the cemetery to drink and socialize. I don't know why we went there, probably because the cops never drove through there.

Boyfriends weren't allowed in the dorm rooms. We had a curfew of 10 PM during the week and 11 PM on Friday and Saturday nights. We were always mindful of the time when we were on a date or out with our friends. The house-mother locked the door at the designated curfew time, and there was no getting back in once the door was locked unless the student crawled in through the window.

To enter and leave the dorm, you had to walk past the housemother. She had a watchful eye, and very little got past her. Our first dorm mother was the sweetest lady ever. We all loved her. She was a beautiful older woman who always wore her hair in a bun with a pencil stuck in it and a silver charm bracelet that jingled when she moved. She wore that charm bracelet so we could hear her coming allowing us time to correct something we weren't supposed to be doing. After a year she worked only on weekends and we had to break in a new one. For some reason we just didn't take a liking to her as much. It seemed we were always scheming to aggravate her. One of the girls really drove the new house mother crazy, and my roommate and I covered for her. I will call her "the mischievous one." She was always pulling the fire alarm. She would fill her bathtub with water, pull the alarm, then run and jump into her tub. When the house mother came charging though the hall and into the rooms, our friend was in the bathtub; it couldn't have been her that sounded the alarm. After several pulls, it was brought to the attention of the administration that the alarm only sounded in the dorm. This was rewired so that the hospital would also be alerted.

There were three telephones in the entire dorm. The one on the second floor for was for local calls. The house mother had one in her office that we used occasionally and for emergencies. The other one was in a telephone booth that was located in the hallway near the parlor. We crammed as many bodies as we could get into that phone booth trying to beat some sort of record. Once I called my boyfriend stationed in Korea from that phone booth. I inserted twenty-five dollars' worth of quarters in the slot for a three-minute conversation.

A dorm room inspection committee, consisting of the house

mother and a couple of students, came around for surprise inspections every so often. These were never really a surprise because somebody always told, making sure the students had time to clean up and hide any alcohol. I was on the committee one year. All and all, we kept our living quarters neat and clean, some better than others.

At the first inkling of warm weather, usually in March, we put on our bikinis, crawled out of the second story window onto "tar beach" to lay in the sun. We lay on the roof with our bodies slathered in a mixture of baby oil and iodine transforming ourselves from student nurses to "sun goddesses." We set a transistor radio in the window sill, turning it up as loud as it would go. Sometimes there would be nine or ten of us soaking up the rays unknowingly damaging our skin, but we looked good with our tan bodies, and *that* was a priority.

Not every freshman had a car, but most of the upperclassmen did. We parked them on the street parallel to the curb in front of the student dorm. The most famous car was a '64 Chevy II Nova named Irena. Irena didn't have air conditioning, but she sported a great radio. No telling how many miles we rode singing along with John Denver, our favorite.

One day we were in our dorm room, when Irena's owner jumped up and ran down the stairs to the street. She recognized the familiar sound of the engine. Someone had hot-wired and stolen Irena. Fortunately, the Nova was found and returned to her owner unharmed.

We took turns driving our cars in town usually to one of the few restaurants. Being a mill town, there were many railroad tracks that we crossed frequently. One of our dorm friends had a stick-shift Beetle that spit and sputtered at times. One night, three of us were riding in the Beetle when we saw a train coming. She decided to beat the train. Just as the front two wheels were across the railroad track the Beetle went dead. There I was in the backseat with no door yelling, "Get out! Get out!"

The driver nervously tried cranking the bug. Finally, the engine turned over and we sputtered away. That was a close call—too close—one I will never forget.

As most freshmen do living away from home, there comes a time for them to "spread their wings." We were only there a month when four of us decided to do something exciting and sort of "sneaky."

October is a "Fair" month in the south and it was the week of the Chattahoochee Valley Fair in Columbus, Georgia. One of our classmates lived near there and asked a few of us to go. We cooked up a plan. After class we piled into her '68 Camaro and headed to the state line. Three of us were eighteen and only one of us was nineteen, the legal age in Georgia.

Once we arrived at our classmate's home we unloaded our bags and headed to the fair. On our way we stopped at a liquor store, pooled our money and the oldest one bought some alcohol to take back to Alabama. We had a great time at the fair, getting in late, and getting up early to make it back to the junior college for class. We were within a mile of the college when a man driving a white car crossed the center line hitting us head on. The Camaro held up and protected us from injury. But what about the alcohol on board? Surely, the police would come, and maybe a photographer from the local paper. I envisioned a picture of the wreck with us on the front page. *What if my mama and daddy found out?*

Luckily, we were saved by our new friend, the male student. He, too, was driving to class when he came upon our accident. We discreetly transferred the illegal bottles to his car before the police came. Now, if we could escape the newspaper reporter. Luckily, the incidence was kept quiet. We didn't try anything like that again for quite a while.

The annual Halloween party was held yearly on October 31st in the basement of the nursing dorm. Most of us participated. Our first Halloween my roommate and I made our own costumes; Raggedy Ann and Andy. Our wigs were made of red yarn. The Sani White shoe polish was the perfect make-up. After the official party we drove over to a friend's house where we continued the celebration.

❧❧

My class was the only group of residents housed in the dorm in the summer of '74. There were about twenty of us. We did clinicals in the hospital perfecting our nursing skills. There was a park nearby where we went many evenings. It was a safe place and cooler than our dorm rooms. Hundreds of small lights decorated the big trees, making it a beautiful site. We loved to hang out there. By now we were knowledgeable of the town and felt safe, but didn't go out and about alone; usually three or four of us stayed together. Occasionally one of our married classmates who lived off campus would invite us to their home for a cook out.

I'm sure my stories are similar to many students that lived in dorms. Yet, our experiences were unique because we were in a small school in a small town and we spent much of our time in the hospital—which was literally at our back door. We had a great view of the emergency room and the doctors' parking lot from our dorm room windows. We knew when things were busy in the emergency room and many times we'd watch out the window. Yes, we were nosey.

"The mischievous one" worked weekends, holidays, and school breaks as a nurse's aide in the hospital so she knew and befriended some of the nursing staff. Because of that, she was "in the know" about things going on in the hospital after our shifts. One evening we got wind of a Cesarean section that was about to take place. Some of us went over, put on scrubs, and observed the surgery. There wasn't an instructor with us. Another time we observed an eye nucleation (removal of the eye) done on a body in the Emergency Room. One of the general surgeons came in that night to harvest her eyes. I will never forget how she looked. Her body was gold and her skin had a metallic glow. Her eyes were open and her face wore a look of fright. It gave me an eerie feeling as we watched him remove her eyes.

For every year I lived in the dorm, there was an unforgettable middle of the night event. The first year, my roommate and I were awakened by a loud banging on our door.

A panicked voice was yelling, "Wake up, come quick", as she ran from door to door for help.

We ran to her room where we found her roommate unresponsive. Knowing she was a diabetic, we figured her condition had something to do with the situation. We quickly picked her up and laid her on a blanket. Barefooted and still in our pajamas, we carried her down the hall, down the stairs, and across the hospital parking lot into the emergency room. We lifted her onto a gurney while her roommate gave her history. A young RN, one of our graduates, returned with a large syringe with a big needle. She stuck it directly into her antecubital vein and administered all of the D50W in the syringe. Our friend immediately responded to the glucose solution. She was surprised when she opened her eyes and saw six wide-eyed girls staring down at her.

She looked around and said, "What are y'all doing?"

She had slipped into insulin shock, or hypoglycemia, and was very lucky her roommate heard her gurgling.

Our second year we were jolted out of bed by the fire alarm. A couple of freshman had set their room on fire. An iron was left on which ignited the curtains and a mattress. We rushed to the room to find the girls crouched in the corner of their smoke-filled room. They were stunned and wouldn't get up, so we physically pulled them out of their room. The fireman came and contained the fire. It was a very exciting night and we had no school the remainder of the week.

Imagine how it feels to be awakened from a dead sleep by the sound of gun shots. That really gets your heart pounding and the adrenalin pumping. I was a senior living on the first floor. My suite-mate and I awoke at the same time. We dove out of our beds and onto the floor when we heard the gun shots so we wouldn't get hit by a flying bullet. *Why would anyone be firing shots at our dorm?* As the gunshots continued we crawled into the hall and slithered up the stairs to the second floor keeping our heads down talking only in a whisper. As the gunshots ceased, we heard laughter. We followed the laughter to find a couple of girls shooting bottle rockets out of the bathroom window. Funny, very funny.

Halloween 1973

Chapter Five

NURSE'S AIDE
1974-1976

After the first semester of nursing school, we were allowed to work as nurse's aides in a hospital. Many of us worked on weekends, holidays, and summer break. It gave us a little spending money as well as an opportunity to practice our skills. I worked any of the eight-hour shifts in the more than thirty-bed hospital in my hometown under the direction of some great registered nurses and licensed practical nurses. One of the nurses who took me under her wing was an LPN by wavier. An LPN by wavier was someone that worked as a nurse's aide or a medic in the military then took the state licensure exam and upon passing, became LPNs. She was a very hard worker assigned to the three-to-eleven shift. Like many of the nurses back then, she was a heavy smoker.

The nurses were very good to me. They took time to teach me things such as how to clean wounds and observed my skills for correctness. Occasionally, when they were busy, they would give me a pill to administer or hang a bottle of IV fluids. The intravenous fluids came in glass bottles and were kept on top of the refrigerator at the nurse's desk. They allowed me to observe their practice—starting IV fluids and administering injections. I learned many of the duties of being a nurse by simply being around them.

As a nurse's aide, I performed routine duties such as TPRs, blood pressures, baths, linen changes, serving meal trays, emptying bedpans and potty chairs. Keep in mind we didn't wear gloves for theses duties. They weren't available like they are today.

I was given an assignment sheet at the beginning of my shift with specific treatments such as enemas or range of motion exercises. On the top of the assignment sheet, the charge nurse would write, OB, ER or nursery. That meant that we were the aide for the entire shift in the assigned department while maintaining our patient assignment. I soon felt like I gave some sort of enema every time I worked; Fleets, mineral oil, or my specialty, soap suds. The liquid soap was mixed with a liter of warm water in a disposable bucket. I had to be careful carrying it to the bedside because it spilled easily. I placed the bucket on the bedside table or hung it from an IV pole. The higher the bucket the faster it went in.

Not all of the patients' rooms were private, but we did have curtains that we pulled to give the patient some semblance of privacy. My most memorable enema encounter involved a very large older woman with "bad knees." I slowly gave the bucket enema with her positioned in bed on her left side, encouraging her to hold it as long as she could. When she could not hold it any longer I got her up holding her close to me trying to transfer her onto the potty chair. She expelled the enema and all that that entailed straight down my leg and into my shoe. That was my initiation for becoming a nurse.

I saw my first GI (gastrointestinal) bleed in this hospital. It was very impressive. The middle-aged man continuously vomited blood while I manually monitored his vital signs and wiped his face with cold cloths. As I dumped the blood filled basin, the nurse administered blood intravenously. The RN inserted a nasogastric tube into his stomach and circulated ice water down the tube. This procedure is known as gastric lavage. She showed me how to do it and I kept the ice water going when she had to leave the patient. It was in the evening and she was the only RN there and responsible for all the patients in the hospital. The bleeding finally slowed. He was a very sick man and was transferred to a larger hospital.

Children were admitted to the hospital with high fevers especially during winter. Some were flushed, dry, crying, and clinging to their parents. Others were lethargic, dozing in and out, they looked so sick. Soon, I learned it was better to have one kicking and screaming than one just lying there. When their fever spiked, they were given aspirin. I gave many alcohol sponge baths to these febrile children. High fever can sometimes cause seizures. I have held glass thermometers under the arms of sick children checking their temperature every thirty minutes. If their fever was dangerously high and we were unable to get it down, the nurse gave them an injection of Pyralgin. It always worked, but later it was discovered that it carried a fatal risk and was no longer prescribed.

While working as an aide, I sat with my first dying patient. She was an unresponsive elderly lady. I didn't know her. The nurse instructed me to sit beside her bed and take vital signs every thirty minutes. Of course, there were no monitors, so I took manual blood pressures and counted her pulse and respirations, writing them down for the nurse. When her blood pressure dropped too low and could no longer be heard with a stethoscope, I palpated her blood pressure. The nurses there taught me how to do that as well. I sat very quietly all afternoon watching the clock, taking her vital signs right on the minute until she faded away. Her family came into her room to check on her, but didn't stay at the bedside. I thought about how she lived and where she'd go when she died.

One evening I was the ER aide when we got a call that a gunshot wound to the head was in route. I was trying to prepare myself for this, not knowing what to expect and I was expecting the worse. I was thinking, "This is gonna be bad." When the patient finally arrived, her face was normal, but she had a small entry wound to her left temple. I cleaned the wound and bandaged it with several rounds of rolled bandage circling her head. After reviewing an x-ray of her head, the doctor told her she was lucky that the bullet had only grazed her skull. He sent her home with instructions not to sleep with a loaded gun under her pillow. I thought, "Do people *really* sleep with a gun under their pillow?"

Because I had lived in this small town all my life, I knew most everybody. Once on ER duty, an older woman came in with paralysis, vomiting, and inability to speak. Her blood pressure was through the roof. This was the first stroke in progress that I had ever witnessed. I'd known her all my life. She was my mother's friend. Her husband was standing there crying, bewildered. I just stood there looking not knowing what to do or say, when the charge nurse yelled out, "Camille, get with it!'

I quickly began taking her vital signs and doing what I needed to do. It was a defining moment for me. *Could I really be a nurse? Could I keep it together and stay focused in any situation?* I've thought about that moment many times—when the going got tough. You have to block it out and do what needs to be done. It's easier said than done. As an older nurse I can still lose it, but it's after the crisis is over. Unfortunately, there was nothing anyone could do for the woman.

One of my high school classmates came to the hospital in labor. I hadn't taken obstetrical nursing in my training, yet, so I'd never seen a birth. I was excited. We took her into the delivery room and called the doctor. He came into the delivery room, put his cigar on the mayo stand, put on his gloves, delivered the baby, took off his gloves, congratulated the new mom, picked up his cigar, and left the room. Watching that baby being born was the most amazing thing I'd ever witnessed.

The RN showed me how to do fundal massage. I stayed with the new mama during her recovery period massaging her uterus and keeping a close watch on her bleeding. A small nursery was across from the nurse's station. I really liked nursery duty which consisted of vital signs, bathing, and feeding the babies.

Over the two and a half years that I worked there I saw many illnesses and injuries. Some passed through the Emergency Room and some were admitted. I observed how the nurses handled situations and conducted themselves with their nursing responsibilities. It made an impression on me greatly influencing my nursing career.

I remember a LPN that was sometimes in charge on the night shift. A woman came in the ER hemorrhaging from vaginal bleeding. The LPN packed her with vaginal packing and saved her life. She did what she had to do.

In nursing school we had instructors close by and in the event of an emergency, the nurses took charge and the student observed. Here, there were many times when I was the one helping the nurse in an emergency or critical situation on the floor.

Time spent here was a great learning experience. I witnessed many *firsts*. Everybody worked together, nurses and nurse's aides.

Winter months were busier than summer months. I had a childhood friend that worked in the lab on the three-to-eleven shifts. Some nights, after the patients were tucked in and the lab was caught up we would sit in the parking lot and listen to the music of a good eight track.

Chapter Six

OB STAFF NURSE
1976–1978

Before graduating I began thinking about where I wanted to work. The options were fairly limited to hospitals, doctor's offices, or nursing homes. Being from a small town, I opted to stay out of big cities. I applied, and was hired as an obstetrical staff nurse making $5.75 per hour at a community hospital in a small river town in Alabama. Like most new graduates, it was a position on the night shift or sometimes called the "graveyard shift."

To help me get on my feet my family gave me some used furniture and I bought a few house hold items. At twenty-one years of age I moved into an apartment thirty miles from my hometown. I paid seventy-five dollars a month for an upstairs apartment in a quad-plex in the middle of town. I knew two people in the whole town, both retired.

I was excited to start my new job as a registered nurse, but hadn't received my state board exam results. I anxiously checked the mailbox every day for six weeks until finally the letter came. PASSED!

৵ৎ

DUTY SHOES

Built in 1975, the community hospital was new and modern. There were no wards and all of the beds were electric. The patient rooms had wall suctions with disposable canisters and piped-in oxygen. No more roll around suctions and big oxygen tanks. The townspeople were very proud of their "new hospital." It was staffed with two family practitioners, a surgeon, an obstetrician, and a radiologist. The seventy-seven bed hospital had a Medical floor, Medical-Surgical floor, Intensive Care Unit, Emergency Room, Surgery, and an Obstetrical Unit.

After a three-month orientation, I began my work on the night shift (11 PM – 7 AM) in the OB department. Until I passed my boards I signed my notes or med sheet as "Camille Foshee TRN, Temporary Registered Nurse. Our time sheets were filled out by the employee and kept in a manila folder in a designated drawer at the nurse's station. Every two weeks they were picked up by the house supervisors who totaled the hours and turned them into the payroll clerk in the administrative office.

The night shift was a big adjustment for me, and I quickly learned some tricks of sleeping in the daytime. First, my bedroom was dark and had an AC window unit to block out all outside noise. Next, I found a breakfast of pancakes, waffles, or biscuits ensured a good day of sleep. I soon learned six hours of sleeping during the day was not the same as sleeping six hours during the night. In order to function, I determined that I needed nine to ten hours of daytime sleep. If I completed my shift on time I was in the bed by 8 AM and usually got up around 5:30 PM. We wore our street clothes in to work and then we changed into hospital issued scrubs.

The hospital obstetrician was an older doctor from New York. In his uniquely personable way, he entered the room, kissed the nurse on the cheek and began his work. Under his direction, I learned some new ways of doing things in labor and delivery. He ordered a pelvimetry on laboring primigravidas. A primigravida, or primip, is a woman pregnant for the first time. A pelvimetry is an x-ray that measures the capacity and diameter of the pelvis. It also shows presentation of the baby, meaning head, feet, or butt turned downward. This helped the doctor decide if the patient could deliver vaginally or if they had an increased need of a Caesarean section. After the perineal shave was done, the patient was given a soap suds enema to clean out the lower colon. Sometimes the

41

enema would augment labor. When the patient was in "good labor" we gave a triple medication injection to help with painful contractions.

The usual medication was Demerol, a narcotic, Vistaril or Phenergan, sedatives, and Scopolamine, an amnesic. This was commonly known as "Twilight Sleep." Often, the Scopolamine, or Scope, caused patients to behave erratically making them difficult to control. I've seen patients take off their gowns, stand up in the middle of the labor bed, and then fall on the mattress like landing on a trampoline. Sometimes they labored naked. We gave up on keeping a hospital gown on them. The older nurses instructed me not to give the whole dose of Scope.

"Just stick the needle in the ampule," they said.

The triple drugs caused the patients to fall asleep only to wake up to painful contractions, crying out and thrashing around in the bed. I can remember women recounting their birth experiences saying, "They gave me a shot, I went to sleep, and when I woke up I was holding my baby." Most did not remember the "in between."

Occasionally, the OB ordered Pitocin, a drug to augment or sometimes start labor. We mixed our own and hung it on an IV pole with no pump. *So, how was it titrated (regulated)?* The OB opened the roll clamp. When he left the room the nurse closed the roll clamp. Too much Pitocin can cause a ruptured uterus and a compromised baby. We were always mindful of that Pitocin and kept it dripping very slowly.

When the OB returned to the patient bedside he asked "What happened to the Pitocin. Why is it so slow?"

We all gave the same answer. "The IV is positional."

Electronic fetal monitoring was new and our unit didn't have it available. Contractions and fetal heart tones were assessed and charted every fifteen to thirty minutes accordingly on the labor record. On the nurses notes we drew a vertical and horizontal line intersecting in the middle (representing a graph of the abdomen.) We marked an "x" in one of the four quadrants of the abdomen where the FHTs were located. A fetoscope was used to auscultate the baby's heartbeat. Similar to a stethoscope, a fetoscope was worn over the doctor's, or nurse's, head and the bell was placed on the mother's abdomen. Soon, I learned how to do vaginal exams for cervical dilatation, and descent of the baby. It was really weird feeling around in there; sometimes I just didn't feel anything. We didn't do cervical exams as often as we do today. These patients didn't have spinals or epidurals, so the nurses could tell much about their progress by the way they acted and their complaints. When one of them said, "I need to push," delivery was usually imminent.

Sometimes, a patient was admitted to the labor room in premature labor. I remember administering alcohol intravenously for premature labor. It made them drunk and sick. Can you imagine mainlining tequila? The alcohol solution came in a glass bottle. We stayed with the patient constantly. The alcohol solution was titrated by the frequency of the contractions. We kept the side rails up and sometimes padded them to keep patients from hurting themselves. If a patient came into the labor room with ruptured membranes, but was not in labor, the doctor ordered a large dose of Penicillin intramuscular. It was kept in the refrigerator on the unit. We gave the injection and sent the patient home.

The OB would always say, "They'll be back."

Usually they returned in labor within a few hours, but sometimes it might be a couple of days.

When the cervix was completely dilated and delivery was close, we transferred the patient to the delivery room by stretcher. We assisted them over to a flat table and positioned their legs in stirrups. The foot of the delivery table dropped and we pushed it under the other half. The legs were strapped to the stirrups and leather wrist cuffs were fastened to keep the mother from touching anything sterile and basically to hold her down. The mother was shown hand bars to hold while pushing.

The RN house supervisor was called for all vaginal deliveries. She administered a nitrous-oxygen mixed gas to help with the pain. I checked the gauge on this machine at the beginning of every shift for accuracy. Even though I was an RN, I did not administer the nitrous-oxygen gas. I wanted no part of that machine. Some of the patients would snore lying flat of their backs waking to push. Trilene was another gas used in the delivery room which was self-administered by the mother. She held the mask to her face, breathed in the gas, and drifted off to sleep. When she fell asleep her hand fell from her face ensuring she did not inhale too much of the gas. If the patient needed some repair on the perineum, the OB stitched the area after an injection with a local anesthetic. Again, there were those rough looking perineums that caused much pain after the deliveries. I thought that was part of having a baby, it was normal. The OB taught us how to deliver a baby, so we would know in case he didn't make it in time.

After the baby was delivered, it was handed to the nurse and placed on its side in a pre-warmed isolette. We dried, suctioned, and stimulated the newborn by rubbing its back with our bare hands. The baby was foot printed and identification bracelets were placed on the newborn and the mother. An Apgar score was assigned at one and five minutes after birth. This is a scoring evaluation for heart rate, respiratory effort, muscle tone, reflex irritability and skin color. The highest score is a ten. The baby was wrapped in warm blankets and taken to the nursery. The father usually saw the baby for the first time through the nursery window or sometimes in the hallway.

Upon arrival to the nursery the newborn was weighed, measured, and assessed for any obvious problems. Silver nitrate was instilled in the eyes as a prophylactic treatment for infection. Silver nitrate was supplied in wax ampules that we opened with a pin. The nurse placed two drops in each eye, and then rinsed with normal saline or sterile water because it was irritating to the their eyes. Vitamin K was injected IM in the thigh to prevent hemorrhagic disease. Temperature was taken rectally with a glass thermometer and recorded as part of the TPR. When warmed, the babies were given a bath. Cord care consisted of painting the base with triple dye, an antiseptic, to prevent infection. If any of the triple dye was spilled it stayed on that surface forever. If it got on our hands it had to "wear off". After a couple hours of observation we gave the babies a bottle of D5W. I can remember some of the big babies emptying the whole four ounce bottle on their first feeding. They loved that sugar water.

After a delivery one of the hospital orderlies came and cleaned the delivery room. An orderly was a male nurse's aide. The mothers were assessed and monitored in recovery before transferring them to a post-partum room.

If the patient needed a Caesarean section, they were taken downstairs to surgery and given general anesthesia by the nurse anesthetist. After delivery, the baby was brought up to the nursery by one of the "surgery girls." There were four of these "surgery girls" and I had the hardest time putting the right face with the right name. They all looked alike in their surgery scrubs. The mamas were recovered in the recovery room then brought up to a post-partum room.

As an OB staff nurse I was responsible for labor and delivery, post-partum, and nursery. A nurse's aide or the OB nurse was in the nursery at all times with the newborns. The vaginally delivered patients remained in the hospital three days and the patients with Caesarean sections stayed longer. Patients having Caesarean sections had a vertical incision of the uterus called a classical incision. The skin incision was also vertical leaving a very obvious scar.

One of the prerequisites for patient discharge after delivery was to have a bowel movement. If they had not had one by discharge time, we gave them a laxative of Milk of Magnesia and Cascara commonly known as "black and white." It worked.

The babies went to their mothers for short visits during the night. Around midnight we weighed, bathed, and assessed vital signs on the babies. Most of the time there were only one or two babies in the nursery, sometimes there were none.

We had two white glass top incubators where the small babies stayed for days, sometimes weeks. It kept a constant warm temperature. Undoubtedly, there are many people walking around today that got a start in one of those incubators. We had fraternal twins that were there for weeks. I named them "Sam and Pam". I see their mother occasionally and she always updates me on what they are up to. They're thirty-eight years old now.

After midnight baths, we wrapped the babies tightly in blankets and rocked them for hours being careful not to fall asleep ourselves. We made "homemade" pacifiers by stuffing gauze in a baby bottle nipple. Sometimes we sang to them. Maybe we spoiled them, but the babies liked it and so did we. If I wasn't up and moving between 4 AM and 5 AM, I struggled to stay awake. The nurses called this period of time "the witching hour."

Obstetric nurses were responsible for replacing supplies and washing instruments. Supplies were brought to the unit from Central Supply. The instruments were soaked in a disinfectant solution and water, scrubbed and rinsed without any use of gloves. There were two large bore needles and glass syringes in the pack.

We were careful to lay them aside. The needles were reusable. Disposable needles and syringes were used only for medication injections. The needles were recapped and thrown in the trash with the syringe. Needles were recapped so the housekeeping personnel wouldn't get stuck. The washed instruments were taken to Central Sterile where they were packaged and sterilized. We never had cause of concern while washing those bloody instruments, we just did it. Disposable gloves were not available, only sterile ones for the doctor and for vaginal checks.

Some nights we had no patients, so I went to other areas of the hospital to help out, usually the emergency room. The ER was staffed with LPNs who were awesome nurses, but sometimes needed a hand with the patient load or IV medications. Some nights were quiet, but not often. There were always patients with headaches, fevers, and minor accidents coming through, as well as heart attacks, major traumas along with other life or death emergencies.

I saw my first heart attack in ER room one. It was late in the shift, around dawn when an older gentleman came in with chest pain and vomiting. His face was so red that in contrast, his white hair seemed to glow. He was sweating profusely. I didn't know *him*, but I did recognize his wife standing at the foot of his gurney. She was one of our nurse's aides. The man went into cardiac arrest, was coded (resuscitative efforts) and died. It all happened so fast.

The hospital doctors staffed the ER and stayed close by for emergencies and nurse calls regarding admitted patients. Pagers weren't available. Many of the patients that came in had to be transferred to other facilities after they were stabilized. Back in the '70s, most rural communities had an ambulance, usually driven by policemen who were also an Emergency Medical Technician (EMT). I had seen and met some of them in and around the ER. Sometimes if the patient's condition warranted a transfer to a larger hospital, a nurse would ride with the patient. Sometimes that nurse would be me.

My first transfer was in February of 1977, a night I'll never forget. When I drove to work that night it was snowing, a rare event in Alabama. A woman presented to the ER with a stroke and needed to be transferred to the city. There were no patients in the OB unit, so I volunteered to go on the thirty mile transfer. It was snowing and fell harder as we left our hospital. Despite the weather we made the trip with no problem.

Upon returning, traveling north on the interstate, we began receiving warnings on the two- way radio that some of the interstate bridges were icing. As we traveled on, we answered a call reporting an accident near mile marker 115 and we were the nearest ambulance. The driver pulled over onto the median, away from the traffic. This part of the interstate had a service road that ran parallel where we were advised the accident occurred. By now it was snowing harder than I'd ever seen. It was dark, freezing, and I was scared. *What would we find?*

My heart pounded as I put on a surgeon's gown over my uniform for warmth. We grabbed a backboard and set out on foot to find the accident. Two policeman carrying flashlights led the way across the median and the southbound interstate. They helped me over a five foot wire fence to make our way down to the wreck.

There it was; an orange Volkswagen Beetle crushed under the cab of a transfer truck. The two vehicles had slid off the interstate onto the service road. There were two passengers in the front seat gasping for breath and bleeding. It was horrible. We couldn't see a backseat. At the same time, two ambulances arrived on the scene accessing the service road. The EMTs pulled out the first passenger and laid her on the hood of the ambulance. She was dead.

They transported the other passenger to the city where she died in route.

We made our way back to the ambulance, stunned at what we'd seen. The policeman drove very slowly back to our hospital as the bridges were icing quickly. As the conditions worsened, the older policeman got out and walked in front of the ambulance pointing out patches of ice to the driver. We made it back safely. The next day, one of the area radio stations reported the accident saying that when the state trooper was completing the report he noticed tennis shoes in the back seat. Unknown to us, there was a ten year old girl in the back seat of the Beetle.

After this harrowing experience, I still rode the ambulance with transfers. Our hospital contracted a city surgeon who began taking some of the ER calls on weekends and covered the hospital for the family practitioners. I knew of him because he had removed my mother's gallbladder in 1968. He was older, maybe early sixties, tall and thin. He was very patient and kind. He worked the weekends that were on my rotation, and he would be the one who gave me instructions on these transfers.

With a pat on the back, he would always say, "Now, Camille, if they die on the way, it's not your fault."

One night a middle-aged man came into the ER complaining of chest pain. He was monitored, assessed and the decision was made to transfer him to a cardiologist in the city. Since there were no monitors on the ambulance, we counted the patient's pulse rate, respirations, and did manual blood pressures during the transfer, which is sometimes difficult to do when the ambulance is in route. The city surgeon gave me a syringe filled with Lidocaine with the instructions to keep my fingers on his pulse and give a prescribed amount of the medicine if his pulse became irregular. Nervously, I kept my fingers on his pulse which remained regular and I did not have to give the Lidocaine. I remember the driver backing into the ambulance bay at the receiving hospital and seeing the sun rise through the back window. Funny how you can recall certain things that seem so insignificant at the time. Luckily, it wasn't his heart, but gallstones. The city surgeon removed his gallbladder a few days later.

Another memorable transfer took place on a very foggy night. The fog was so thick you couldn't see twenty feet ahead. There had been a terrible automobile accident and we were transferring a spinal cord injury. The young man was strapped on to a backboard and couldn't move anything, but his mouth and eyes. He was NPO (nothing by mouth), of course, and so thirsty. He was begging for water. I took a cloth, soaked it in water, wrung it out, and let him suck on it. Our driver was traveling very slowly due to the fog when a tire exploded right before we were tuning onto the interstate ramp. Fortunately, there was no problem stopping the ambulance. We had to wait on the town's second ambulance to arrive. It seemed like hours waiting for it to get there. We transferred the injured man onto the second ambulance and went on our way into the fog. Ambulances aren't known for comfort and smooth ride. I was afraid a jerk or sudden stop might further damage his spinal cord. I rode at the head of the stretcher talking to him while holding his arms. Thankfully, he remained stable the whole way. I always felt like the fog was our friend that night; otherwise, we would have been racing down the interstate when that tire blew.

The ER was the gathering place for the nurses. It had the best coffee in the house and nurses drink a lot of coffee. The nurses station was a six-by-six room where they sat, charted, and smoked. Smoking was allowed throughout the hospital. There was a cigarette vending machine in the hospital lobby. The staff smoked in designated areas adjacent to their units usually the work room or the medicine room. At night some of the nurses and aides smoked at the nurse's desk on the floors. Many of the patients smoked, but were cautioned if there was oxygen flowing in their room. In the ICU, the smokers stood in the door of the medicine room keeping a watchful eye on the patients and the heart monitors.

In the ER you had to be ready for anything that came in the door. Sometimes the ambulance would radio an emergency so we could gather anticipated supplies or meds prior to their arrival. If they called in that a "Code Ten" was in route, the code team would be awaiting their arrival.

Once we were standing around the nurse's station and a pickup truck pulled up at the door and brought in a young man who was DOA with a shotgun blast in his back. The wound was a perfect circle, like a bull's eye. I had never seen anything like that before. I never heard if it was an accidental shooting or if it was intentional.

On the night shift the ER entrance was the only door used, the rest of the hospital's doors were locked. Whenever there was a death during the night the funeral home personnel accessed the hospital through the ER entrance.

One night the director of our local funeral home came to pick up a body. He left the rear door of the hearse open while he came in the hospital. This linebacker-size man came through, spoke to everyone, received the body, and loaded it into the parked hearse. Unknown to him, one of the stray cats that frequented the hospital parking lot had jumped into hearse. The scrawny cat leaped on his back as he drove away. The man burst back through the ER door, pale as a ghost, sweating bullets, and speechless. *Can you imagine how many times that story has been retold?*

There was a security guard on duty during the night shift. Most of them were retired or part time policemen. They made rounds throughout the building periodically, but they mainly stayed in the ER. There was one that the nurses called Barney Fife. He didn't look like Barney Fife, but sometimes acted like him.

Once he was searching his pockets for something and the ER nurse asked him, "What are you looking for?"

He replied, "I can't find my bullet."

He was getting upset because he had lost his bullet. He had just returned from an ambulance run and most likely lost it in the ambulance. An on duty policeman found it and brought it to him. He put the lost bullet in his shirt pocket where it belonged.

During the winter months, the hospital was especially busy. There were a lot of pediatric patients with upper respiratory illnesses, and with those illnesses came croup tents. The nurses and aids had to keep them filled with ice to work properly. When there was an overflow of patients, we converted the ICU waiting room into a patient ward, called "tent city." All of us worked together as a team, helping where ever we were needed. Sometimes I mixed medications for IV's, also called piggybacks, or for the main bags of IV fluid.

Around 5 AM the floors became busy setting the stage for the day. Preps, baths, and labs were done early for surgeries and x-ray studies. Diabetics were awakened to void in a cup for a dipstick glucose.

I learned to start IV lines with intracaths. An intracath consisted of a large bore needle used to enter the vein, upon good blood return, a six-inch catheter was threaded into the vein. The needle retracted into a plastic guard. For some reason starting IVs came easy to me. It has always been my best skill and still is. I always secured the intracath with an arm board wrapping it with kling (an elastic type gauze) and tape. We didn't have IV pumps so we calculated the rate by counting drops.

Occasionally, I went up to the ICU and sat at the desk with nurses who taught me heart rhythms by watching the heart monitors. There were some busy nights on the medical and surgical floors, but usually the medical patients slept. Many of the medical patients were routinely given the sleeping pill Nembutal or Seconal (a highly addictive barbiturates) at bedtime—during second shift— so the patients were sleeping soundly when the night shift came on duty.

Our Director of Nursing was incredible. Everybody loved her. She was such an advocate for nurses. She wore a white uniform and her cap to work every day. Sometimes she came in and hung out with us on the night shift. If we were busy she always helped out.

There was a group of us that gathered at one of our houses for socializing and dinner fairly often. We called our get-togethers, "hen parties." I was the youngest one of the group. Most all of them were smokers, so the kitchen looked like a bar room within thirty minutes. I loved to hear them tell stories of the "old days." After a few drinks, some of them became animated and would make us laugh.

Most of us were a lot alike. You could say we were cut from the same piece of cloth. The biggest difference among us was our ages. Most of us grew up in neighboring counties and some went to the same nursing schools.

I remember a young nurse came from Florida. She sometimes wore her long hair down with feather earrings. She wore different duty shoes too, they were clogs. I had never seen any before. She was different from the rest of us, but she was a good.

Soon I knew every employee on the night shift and made some lifetime friends. I felt a part of the hospital family which was very important to me. I went to my first hospital wide picnic that fall. It was at the National Guard Armory. The night shift employees worked hard on their skit that was performed at the picnic. We made characters from large cardboard boxes on which we painted faces and placed crepe paper hair. The arms were stuffed shirts worn over our hips. As the music began we strutted onto the stage and went out into the audience. We even grabbed a man by the arm to come up and dance. It was hilarious.

After a year and a half of nights, I had an opportunity to move to a day charge nurse position working the Medical-Surgical floor. The hospital was initiating a new schedule seven-days-on, seven-days-off with eight-hour shifts. I loved working with the mothers and babies, but I had gotten married and still struggled with the night time hours, so I took the position.

Hospital Picnic

Chapter Seven

CHARGE NURSE, MEDICAL SURGICAL NURSING 1978-1979

In the spring of 1978 I became the charge nurse on the thirty-three bed medical surgical floor. I looked forward to working with new people and learning new responsibilities. I had worked with the doctors on the night shift and they knew me by name. There were two family practitioners that admitted the majority of patients. The older one became my family doctor until he retired. He and his nurse always took good care of me and my girls—they love him.

The other physician had a large practice and kept a high census of hospital patients. He is still practicing today and is presently my doctor. Then, there was the hospital surgeon. He was loud, direct and intimidating, but over the years I learned his bark was much worse than his bite. He taught me the importance of obtaining a thorough patient history. An orthopedic surgeon who came from the city operated on Wednesdays. The OB/GYN did some gynecological surgeries. This group of doctors kept the hospital full and busy. When a patient was admitted and a chart was compiled, a colored piece of tape was placed on the chart to differentiate each doctor making the charts easier to identify. There were only five rolls of tape on our tape dispenser, pink, yellow, red, white, and blue.

My eight hour shift started at 6:45 AM with report from the night shift nurses. Our hospital utilized the team nursing concept so all of the staff listened to report while the nurses made notes on each patient. I wrote assignments for the nurse's aides, being mindful of the bed bound or total care patients. After report, I immediately went into each room to meet the patients and to put a face with the name. I started with room 201 and ended with room 225. The even numbered rooms were semi private meaning there were two beds in each room and the patients shared a bathroom. The odd numbered rooms were private.

Upon returning to the desk there was usually one of the family practitioners making rounds and I caught up with him. I rounded with one of the doctors off and on during the morning. It was important to make rounds to know the patient complaints and the doctor's response to those complaints. I also read their orders as they wrote them, making sure they were legible. It took me awhile to learn to read their handwriting especially the young family practice doctor. I asked questions *then*, instead of phoning them later but over time I learned to read his orders with ease. Often times, the patients had questions about what the doctor had said and it was always good to have heard the conversation for myself so that I could explain things to them.

I always rounded with the hospital surgeon, pushing the dressing cart behind him into each room. He was high maintenance. He dressed the wounds and incisions himself. I opened the sterile supplies as he called for the item he needed. For the most part, he didn't wear sterile gloves or any gloves for that matter to do the dressing changes. He always washed his hands between patients. Once he and I were changing the dressing of a below the knee amputation when he asked for kerlix. I replied timidly, "What's kerlix?"

He bellowed, "What's kerlix? You don't know what kerlix is?"

I scrambled quickly down the hall and brought back an armful of kerlix. I learned that lesson and from then on I knew the name of everything on the dressing cart and checked it every morning making sure everything was there.

Sometimes the hospital surgeon had consults on the medical

floor. If the charge nurse of the medical floor knew he was coming up there she would quickly get busy in a room down the hall. She didn't deal with him unless she absolutely had to. He, of course, caught on to that and would purposely aggravate her.

Labs and x-ray results were put in a wire basket at the nurse's station. After lunch I sat down at the desk and reviewed these results calling the doctor if needed, and then the ward clerk posted them on the chart.

The nurses loved the new seven-days-on, seven-days-off schedule. My team worked every other weekend and was plenty busy. Normally tests were done during the week and only emergency surgeries were performed. The hospital surgeon rounded every weekend on his patients and the rest of the patients were seen by one of our on-call doctors or the city surgeon. It so happened that the city surgeon worked on my weekend so I rounded with him. He explained different illnesses and I learned a lot from him. When rounds were finished he always patted me on the back and gave me a complement about my work. Once he said to me, "I'll sign whatever you write." He knew I would never order anything more than a diet or a dose of Mylanta. He smoked while he rounded, leaving the cigarette in an ash tray on top of the chart rack when he went into patient rooms.

The charge nurse mixed intravenous medications in the medicine room behind the nurse's station. The piggybacks were usually antibiotics. We added potassium chloride or vitamins to the liter bottles. The vitamins left yellow stains if any squirted on your uniform. RNs labeled the solutions with red labels including the patient name, room number, medication, date and time with our initials. I administered IV push medications always taking two minutes to infuse the drugs. The two most common medications I gave intravenously were Lasix and Solu-Medrol. I made sure I didn't push any medicine into a line with another medication. I recall Valium being one that clouded when mixed with other medications. That happened to me once and I never forgot it. I gave the drug Hyperstat rapidly IV push to treat patients in a "hypertensive crisis." It worked immediately. I soon learned the compatibility of commonly used medications. I was very particular giving IV medications. I certainly didn't want to kill anybody.

I completed admission paperwork and assessments on new

patients. If an IV was ordered I started IV fluids. The hospital began using a short catheter called a cathlon for IVs. They were easier to place and came in different sizes. The smallest cathlons were twenty four gauge. They were used on infants, children and the elderly with tiny veins. The largest was an eighteen gauge that was used on surgery patients and those who needed blood transfusions. The cathlons were color coded just as they are today.

No day on the Medical-Surgical unit was ever the same; we rolled with the needs of the patients. There was always something new to learn, a new diagnosis or an unfamiliar surgery. Sometimes patients required one-on-one care and there were days when I stayed at a bedside for hours. Often, a sick surgery patient would return to the floor after a complicated case which was usually some sort of bowel surgery with tubes everywhere, multiple IVs, and a huge dressing and a full page of orders.

I would say to other nurses, "Why didn't they go to ICU?"

On occasion a surgical patient would go to ICU, but the hospital surgeon repeatedly said, "I want my patients, on my floor, with my nurses looking after them." And that's what we did.

That year I learned to insert NG tubes. If the patient could drink water they went down fairly easy, but for the confused patient it was a nightmare. They were always pulling them out—a natural reaction. If I couldn't get them back down after one attempt I called my house supervisor who was the NG tube expert. She had a knack for those things. NG tubes were put down as feeding tubes especially for patients who couldn't swallow. These were typically stroke patients.

As I recall Ensure was the first commercial feeding that we used for these patients. It was given as bolus feeding in a 60cc syringe. Afterwards the tube was flushed with water to keep it open. If one became clogged we used Coca-Cola to clear the tube.

We also inserted NG tubes to decompress the abdomen. The NG tube was connected to an intermittent suction keeping the stomach empty. I have inserted them before, connected it to suction and returned to the patient to find the canister filled with some sort of sediment. I questioned myself, "Is that poop?" If it looks like poop and smells like poop, it's poop. Yes, this can happen with bowel obstructions. I didn't know this was possible until I saw it for myself.

These patients were referred to the hospital surgeon and were operated on to repair the problem. Of course, the hospital surgeon had a special red rubber NG tube we were instructed to use on his patients. We put it on ice for a few minutes to make it stiff and easier to insert

Once, I inserted an NG tube into a friend of mine. His wife, a nurse, stood by the bedside holding his hand. I inserted it into his nose, but it went up instead of down—like it should have. I think I stuffed it into his sinuses. His face turned blood-red and he started coughing. He couldn't talk. His wife and I were laughing so hard. He jerked that tube out and spoke a few choice words. Needless to say, he didn't let me try that again and to this day he reminds me of the episode.

RNs administered blood transfusions. We took the chart to the lab with us to get the blood which was kept in a special refrigerator in the lab and was signed out with a lab technician. Two nurses always checked the patient information against the blood labels for correctness. I stayed at the bedside for the first fifteen to twenty minutes after the blood was started, then kept a close watch on the patient until the transfusion was complete. Usually, if there is a blood reaction it happens within the first fifteen minutes. I've only seen it once and it happened shortly after beginning the transfusion. All at once the patient started shaking, his fever spiked to 103 and the urine in his Foley catheter became bloody. I immediately stopped the blood, called for help, took vital signs and called the doctor. I was afraid that he was going to die, but he didn't.

The two LPNS I worked with were wonderful. They were "seasoned nurses" who showed me the ropes. One worked the surgical east wing of the floor and the other, the medical west wing of the floor. They administered PO (by mouth) medications, gave most of the IM medications, hung IV fluids and piggybacks. They did most of the decubitus ulcer (bed sores) and wound care which could be very time consuming. They managed the NG tube feedings.

LPNs did most of the charting in the nurses notes and on the graphic sheet for vital signs. The day shift charted in blue or black, evening shift in green and the night shift in red. Each LPN was responsible for their medication cart. The carts had individual patient drawers that were changed out twice a day. The larger top drawer was under lock and key and contained narcotics. These controlled substances were counted at the beginning and the end of each shift with the outgoing and incoming nurse. There was always a large jar of Vaseline on the carts. It was used in the treatment of diverticular disease. The nurse mixed the Vaseline with applesauce and gave it to patients as part of their medication regimen.

Scheduled surgery patients were admitted the day before surgery for lab work, a chest x-ray and an EKG. The east end LPN and I readied them for surgery, getting their consents signed, shaving the operative site and often administering an enema. An hour before their scheduled surgery the patients were given a pre-operative dose of Demerol, Vistaril and Atropine intramuscularly. The Demerol and Vistaril sedated the patient and the Atropine dried up secretions. Their IVs were usually started in the holding area in surgery.

The floor was staffed with four nurse's aides and an orderly, or male attendant. I don't know what the team would do without them. They performed their assignments with little instruction. Most of them were older and things were different back then so they took a lot of time with their patients.

One male attendant was a practical joker. When urine specimens were collected they were brought to the desk, labeled, and taken to the lab. One day I was standing at the counter and noticed the attendant bring a specimen to the counter, label it, take the top off and drink it. *What?* It totally caught me off guard. He had poured apple juice in that particular container.

The nurse's aides turned and repositioned bed bound patients every two hours. They paid particular attention to the skin care of incontinent patients and reported any skin breakdown to the nurses. During the school year, a DO (Diversified Occupation) student came in after lunch picking up duties of the nurse's aides. Many of these students became nurses.

The Unit Secretary or Ward Clerk stayed at the nurse's station to answer phone calls, order supplies and transfer doctor's orders onto the MAR (Medication Administration Record) and the cardex. The MAR had the medications listed and the cardex entries were other orders. Entries written on the cardex were done in pencil so they could be erased for updating. The nurses signed the orders after the unit secretary transcribed them. The doctor's order sheet had a carbon copy that was pulled and sent to the pharmacy via the dumbwaiter in the medication room. Each patient had a blue plastic card—kind of like a credit card—with their information on it. We kept them in order—according to room number—in a holder by the addressograph machine. This machine had a rolling ink pad that labeled the patient's record. These cards were used in stamping the chart record, charges and requests by the Unit Secretary. After 9 PM the unit secretary became the switchboard operator.

Even though each team member had their own responsibilities, we always worked together and helped one another. No one was ever above any task. I never asked them to do anything that I wouldn't do myself.

The nurses and the nurse's aides wore white uniforms and the nurses wore their caps. We mainly wore dresses with white support hose. The unit secretary wore white and royal blue. The DO students dressed in pink uniforms. In our pockets were bandage scissors, a writing pen, tape, and alcohol swabs. A wrist watch with a second hand wrapped our wrist and a stethoscope draped our necks. I kept my hair up off my collar usually in a ponytail or braid. I never wore fingernail polish or perfume.

Upon admission, each patient was given a disposable admission kit consisting of a wash basin, a water pitcher, and a glass mercury thermometer. Most patients received a blue tip thermometer, but those requiring rectal temperatures received a red tipped one. Most patients loved the wash basins and carried them home to shell peas and butterbeans during the summer. Supplies including bedpans were disposable; we dusted them with powder to keep from sticking to the patient. We instructed the patient regarding use of the nurse call light and the three channel television set. Very little was discussed with the patient about their plan of care, as that was done by the doctor. Discharge instructions weren't much more than "when to return to the doctor." The doctor gave the patient prescriptions as he wrote them at the bedside. When nursing home patients were discharged, the doctor made a phone call and the patient was sent back usually by ambulance. The family practitioner continued their care in the nursing home. Discharged homebound patients could receive home health services with a referral by the hospital social worker.

Back then, just as today, hand washing was the number one

way to prevent infection. Each patient room had a sink with a soap dispenser and paper towels on a roll crank. I washed my hands so much my fingers cracked open.

Disposable gloves were not readily available, but if we ever came across a box they were "one size fits all" and were more trouble than they were worth, so we didn't bother. Each medicine cart had a red needle box, or "sharp's container," on it where needles were disposed. If we were down the hall away from the needle box we recapped the needles and threw them away in the trash can or put them in our pocket.

The most careless thing we did involved the IV tray that the nurses took from room to room. The plastic tray was carried by a handle located over the top and the supplies were kept in the tray. Some of the nurses put dirty needles in the bottom of the tray or stuck them in the side. Once in a while, we cleaned the tray, removing the dirty needles and disposed of them in the cardboard box that the syringes were packaged in.

I had good post-operative training in nursing school so I was somewhat familiar with most of the surgeries admitted to our floor. The hospital surgeon did many abdominal operations which involved opening the abdominal cavity usually due to a disease process. He did some surgeries due to trauma such as splenectomies (removal of spleen). Probably the most common surgery he did was a cholecystectomy, or removal of the gallbladder. It was very painful due to the location of the five inch incision under the rib cage. It hurt them to breathe. They usually had a three to five day hospital stay. Appendectomies had the easiest recovery, but it was still hard to get some of them up. Most of the time, grown men were the hardest to get up and moving after surgery. Some of the "big abdominal surgeries" were the bowel resections and colostomies. They returned to the floor with an NG tube, IV fluids, piggybacks and a Foley catheter. We kept all the tubes patent and the drainage containers emptied. Strict records of intake and output was essential in the care of surgery patients.

A big bulky dressing hid the long vertical abdominal incision. The heavier patients had "stay" or retention sutures along with skin sutures. The retention sutures were made of thick heavy suture that held the layers of incision together. They were removed in ten to fourteen days. Many times there was a Penrose drain inserted during surgery that was shortened postoperatively with the dressing changes. Sometimes we applied Montgomery straps to a patient whose dressing needed frequent changes. Montgomery straps consisted of two identical pieces of bandage. The sticky part adhered to the skin on each side of the dressing and the non-adhesive part had holes that laced up over the dressing. It reminded me of a corset. This would help to keep the incision closed for proper healing.

The surgeon had us use Bongort bags on the colostomies. We had to cut them to match the size of the stoma, peel the backing and stick them to the skin around the stoma. They always leaked and the colon contents badly irritated the skin. Some of the lucky patients were able to have their colostomies reversed which meant another abdominal surgery in three to six months to re-anastomose or reconnect the colon. Sometimes the patients would return to the floor with a loop of bowel pulled to the outside of the abdominal cavity. A glass rod held the bowel outside. A few days later, in the patient's room, the surgeon cut the colon making a double barrel colostomy or two stomas.

This was the case with a mentally challenged patient. The morning after surgery we entered the patient's room during rounds; I noticed her sitter had fallen asleep at the bedside. I thought, *that's not good.*

The surgeon took off the dressing, examined the wound and redressed it with another bulky dressing. When we left the room I said to him, "She's gonna pull that rod out."

He replied, "No, she won't."

A few hours later, I was at the nurse's desk and I saw the patient waddling down the hall. She was holding her colon in her hand. What a sight. I excitedly called the surgeon reporting what had happened, adding that little, "I told you so," before I hung up the phone. We got her back to bed, and laid sterile saline soaked gauze over the bowel. The surgeon quickly came and stuffed it back in. Unbelievable.

The colon surgeries were a big production. The patients were admitted three days before the scheduled operation for preparation of the bowel which included a clear liquid diet, antibiotics by mouth, laxatives and enemas. After the surgery, bowel sounds were hesitant to resume. I listened all over the abdomen to hear some kind of "tinkling in the gut." The nurses administered Ilopan IM for gas discomfort. Finally the bowel woke up, the NG tube was removed and the patient was allowed to drink some liquids. The surgeon gradually advanced their diet. I recall thinking to myself, "I hope I never have to have one of these operations. They're awful!"

The worst abdominal surgery and post-operative care were those with an abscess or multiple abscesses. Those patients had some wicked wounds and the odor was indescribable. We did scrounge up some gloves for this type of wound care. When I was pregnant I just couldn't handle these dressing changes; the odor was too much. These patients were always very sick and required massive doses of antibiotics. They stayed in the hospital for weeks.

Thyroidectomy patients were brought back to the floor accompanied by the recovery room nurse and a tracheotomy (trach) tray. The trach tray was left at the bedside in the event swelling occurred causing difficulty breathing. I dreaded the day one of these patients would need an emergency trach. Thank, "goodness," that never happened on my shift.

The post-op care of amputations bothered me. My daddy was an amputee. I knew that these patients would have phantom pain the rest of their lives and would have to adjust to life without a limb. Phantom pain is felt after the amputation of a limb, having the sensation that the limb is still there. On the other hand, I've seen some rotten feet in my career: Sometimes amputation is the only solution.

The orthopedic surgeon scheduled operations weekly and performed emergency surgeries when needed. He did joint replacements and repaired broken bones. I liked taking care of his patients and was always mindful of the limitations associated with this kind of surgery.

I admitted a young woman for a total knee replacement scheduled for the next morning. I was off the next day so I made arrangements to observe her surgery. I'd always wanted to observe a total joint replacement. My mother in law was the surgery supervisor so I got the "okay." I arrived early and talked with the patient before she went into the operating room. After everyone and everything was positioned I went into the operating room standing in a spot where I could see. Well into the surgery, I began to feel a little queasy. I took some deep breaths through the surgical mask trying to shake it off. Then I felt hot, sweaty and nauseated. I thought I was going to pass out; I had to leave the room. I didn't go back. It wasn't only seeing the surgery, but hearing the sounds of the equipment being used that made me weak at the knees. I could never be a surgery nurse.

The OB/GYN did gynecological surgeries, including abdominal hysterectomies, tubal ligations, dilations and curettages (D&C). Unbelievably, husbands had to sign permits for female sterilization. Patients receiving abdominal hysterectomies had vertical incisions and returned to the floor with Foley catheters. They usually stayed in the hospital three to five days. The tubal ligations and D&Cs were admitted the day before their surgeries and were readied by the nurses on the floor. They were discharged the day after surgery.

As soon as the surgical patients were awake enough to follow instructions they were told to turn, cough, and breathe deeply to prevent pneumonia. There was little done to prevent the formation of blood clots back then. The general surgeon, or the nurses, wrapped the patient's legs with ace bandages starting at the toes and ending at the knees. We usually got the patients up the day after surgery. The term *pain management* was unheard of; however, we did give narcotics intramuscularly every three to four hours. Mepergan was the drug of choice. This was a combination of Demerol and Phenergan. It's no longer available in the United States.

There were some tough surgeries with big incisions and a limited availability of pain medicines. Not only was pain an issue, but due to the type of general anesthetics given and the surgery itself, many patients experienced extreme nausea. Phenergan, Compazine, and Tigan suppositories were given to combat the nausea.

There were no outpatient surgeries done other than removal of a mole or some type of skin lesion. These minor cases were usually done in the ER.

There were more medical patients on my floor than surgical patients. The majority of the medical patients were cared for by the family practitioners, but sometimes the surgeon had a few as well.

Some patients were admitted for tests. At the time, our hospital diagnostic capabilities consisted of lab work, x-rays and

63

electrocardiograms (EKGS). There was a radiologist in house that read all of our x-rays. Upper GI studies and Barium enemas used Barium as the contrast medium. "Enemas until clear" were given by the nurse's aides beginning around four in the morning the day of a scheduled test. After the barium study a big dose of Milk of Magnesia (MOM) was given to expel the barium. An x-ray of the gallbladder, or Cholecystogram, was done with the use of a contrast medium such as Telepaque. One hour after the evening meal of the night before the test, six Telepaque tablets were given orally every five minutes. Gallstones were revealed on the x-ray as mottled densities in the gallbladder.

Many chronic "lungers", as they were known, were admitted for the exacerbation of emphysema or COPD (Chronic Obstructive Pulmonary Disease). Typically they smoked two packs of cigarettes a day and had a chronic cough. Many of them had yellow fingers stained from holding cigarettes. Upon getting any type of upper respiratory infection they became short of breath, fatigued, wheezed and coughed up some nasty looking stuff spitting it in their emesis basin that we kept emptied. We treated them with antibiotics, breathing treatments, steroids, and the bronchodilator, Theophylline. Usually the patient recovered from the episode, went home, continued the two-pack a day habit and returned with the same scenario every few months especially in the winter time. There were other lung conditions that filled hospital beds such as pneumonia and bronchitis.

Patients with conditions of the heart were admitted also. The most common of these was CHF, or congestive heart failure. We treated them with Lasix, a diuretic, and Digitalis, an antiarrhythmic. These patients were monitored closely for electrolyte imbalances and toxic effects of the digitalis.

I will never forget one patient with CHF. He was a tall, big man. He was frequently in and out of the hospital with shortness of breath and edema. Each time he came into the hospital, his nose and his ears appeared bigger. For some reason I was the one that walked him to the end of the hall and back to his room. Every step he took required a huge effort. He was miserable, sitting and wearing oxygen all day. I felt bad for him. I assumed his CHF resulted from a previous heart attack. Each time I walked with him I said a little prayer for my daddy, who had a heart attack. I prayed he'd never end up like this man.

Our hospital treated many individuals suffering from heart attacks. Some of them were transferred to a cardiac unit in the city while others were admitted to our ICU. Barring any further complications, once the patient became stable they were transferred to the medical floor. The key element in the nursing care of these patients was physical and emotional rest. These patients usually had a hospital stay of at least two weeks.

We treated children and adults diagnosed with pneumonia with IM Penicillin. Within twenty-four hours their fever would be down and they could eat and drink. The response to Penicillin—a miracle drug—was fast and remarkable.

Frequently, patients were confused, combative and were prone to hurt themselves. At times there was a spouse at the bedside who was not capable of looking after the patient. And sometimes there was no caregiver with the patient. We used wrist restraints and a posey vest to restrain these patients. The restraints were ordered by the doctor, but no special order or charting was required to use them as is the case today.

Alcoholics were admitted often to our floor with alcohol related diagnoses. We gave some of them paraldehyde for alcohol withdrawal. This medicine was given immediately after it was poured and measured because it reacted with plastic and would eat a hole in the dosage cup. It smelled terrible. I couldn't believe people drank that stuff. Some alcoholics were given a shot of whisky in the evening to prevent alcohol withdrawal and delirium tremors, or DTs. I recall a patient suffering from DTs that was hallucinating. The staff tried to physically restrain him and I got too close and was kicked in the abdomen. I was pregnant, but I kept going.

Frequently, we had patients who presented with a spontaneous pneumothorax (collapsed lung). Chest tubes were placed when the patient arrived to unit. The chest tube was put into the pleural space of the chest to re-expand the lung. The hospital surgeon inserted and managed the chest tubes. Much emphasis was placed on protection of the gallon glass bottle taped to the floor that contained the water seal drainage. A large surgical clamp was at the bed side at all times to clamp the tube if the tubing or the bottle became damaged. I was always mindful of that bottle and only got near it when I had to measure the drainage at the end of the shift. I could only imagine the repercussions of breaking one of those glass bottles.

Patients requiring total care had no special beds or mattresses as they do today, but *our* hospital beds were electric, making positioning much easier for the patient and the personnel.

Draw sheets were placed on top of the bottom flat sheets to help with pulling patients up to the head of the bed and repositioning them. We placed sheep skin pads under patients and applied sheep skin heel pads in an effort to prevent decubitus ulcers, or pressure sores. Most incontinent patients had an indwelling Foley catheter. We checked them often for bowel incontinence keeping their skin coated with Vaseline. Often a footboard was placed at the foot of the bed to prevent foot drop. The hospital physical therapist did range of motion exercises on these patients as ordered. This helped prevent contractures, a stiffening of the joints.

A young OB/GYN came to town in the fall of '78, setting up practice with rest of the doctors in the medical office building next to the hospital. He moved his family and his Ferrari from California. He built his practice quickly. He brought new techniques with him being the first doctor to perform laparoscopic surgery at our hospital with bilateral tubal ligations and exploratory laparotomies. These early laparoscopes didn't have cameras with a big screen. Therefore, the doctor had to stand over the patient looking through an eyepiece. This was new to us nurses.

Many of his hysterectomies were done vaginally. These women returned to the floor without an abdominal incision, but had a supra pubic catheter connected to a drainage bag that collected urine. The OB called it a Banano catheter. I thought the bulb holding it in place must be shaped like a banana hence the name. When doing my research I discovered Banano originated from the named of the doctor that designed it.

The new doctor in conjunction with the hospital wanted to offer prenatal classes for expecting parents and needed a couple of nurses to teach. My friend and I volunteered .The hospital flew us to Miami to a childbirth seminar to receive certification to teach the class. I was twenty-five weeks pregnant at the time, expecting my first child. We learned all about childbirth, breathing and relaxation techniques. While in Miami I experienced some tugging in my side but passed it off as pregnancy related. We returned home and I went to work as usual, but I couldn't stand up straight without pain in my right lower quadrant. After a quick assessment and lab work, the hospital surgeon diagnosed me with appendicitis. I'd fallen victim to the "NURSE CURSE!"

I was sent to my OB in the city who concurred with the diagnosis and was about to call in a surgeon whom I'd never heard of. I asked him to call the city surgeon whom I knew. I was admitted to the big hospital where I knew no one. I was so scared and worried about my baby. Shortly, the city surgeon came in and checked my abdomen. He sat down beside me and told me that if my appendix burst that both of us could die. He explained that I would not be put to sleep until he was ready to operate which would shorten the anesthesia time. With a familiar pat on the back he told me that everything was going to be alright. Hearing him say that was the reassurance I needed to get through this risky surgery. I knew I was in good hands and he'd take care of me.

As I lay on the operating table waiting, I prayed that God would see us through this ordeal. When I woke up in the recovery room I felt her kick. That was her way of saying to me, "Mama, I'm okay." I recovered nicely, but was left with a four-inch incision on my pregnant belly. At twenty-three that scar was devastating.

"How am I ever gonna wear a bikini again?" I asked at my post-op appointment.

He said "Just wear your bikini, don't worry about it, nobody will even notice."

This was the first time I'd been the patient instead of the nurse. I didn't like it and in a few weeks I would be the patient again.

I went into labor around 4 AM. The regular contractions weren't too bad so I took my time showering to shave my legs. My husband and I arrived at shift change, 7 AM, at the big hospital in the city. This particular morning the unit was very busy and there were no labor rooms available. I labored on a Gurney behind one of the portable green screens in the hall by an exit to the stairs. Everybody that went in or out of that door made an effort to look behind the screen.

Upon admission the lab girl came to draw blood. She was about to stick me as I was obviously having a contraction so I asked her, "Are you going to stick me while I'm having a contraction?"

She reluctantly loosened the tourniquet and stepped back. I never forget that and I never stick a patient while they're having a contraction.

I received a perineal shave and my first and only soap suds enema. They made me hold the whole thing. I thought I was gonna die.

I used the breathing and relaxation techniques that I'd taught in childbirth classes in order to get through the first few hours of contractions. Around 11 o'clock I was about to come apart with pain. I cried softly, but never yelled out.

When I asked the nurse for my epidural, she told me I had to wait until I was four centimeters dilated. The contractions were coming one right after another. I didn't think it could get any worse when my water broke which intensified my pain even more. The fluid was running off the gurney onto the floor.

"Please. Please can I get my epidural?" I begged.

Finally, the OB came to my bedside and administered the epidural which gave me great relief.

I remember him saying to me, "its 12:30 and I haven't been to the office yet."

When I was completely dilated the nurses rolled me into the delivery room and pulled me onto the delivery table. As they were about to strap my wrists in the restraints I told them that I was a nurse and promised that I wouldn't touch anything sterile if they would leave my hands free. They honored my request.

I looked up into a mirror mounted to the ceiling and I saw a pair of forceps. They were coming out of me! I couldn't watch. He delivered my six pound eight ounce baby girl with forceps and a fourth degree episiotomy.

I heard her cry and saw her briefly as the doctor held her up. The nurses placed her in an isolette and rolled her by me as my husband followed.

After the stitch work, I was rolled into the recovery area where I began shaking uncontrollably. The warm blankets they piled on top of me didn't help; I wasn't cold. I've learned in my experience that this shaking was probably due to fluid and blood loss during delivery. Not every woman does this after delivery.

I was taken to a semi-private room that I shared with a teenage mother.

Finally, I got to hold my baby. In an instant all the love in the whole world was right there in my arms. She was beautiful. My heart was full as I held her close and looked at her sweet little face. It was the happiest day of my life.

We stumbled our way through the first breast feeding. Soon, the epidural faded and the pain came. It was awful. During my three days in the hospital, I shamefully asked for pain medicine and looked forward to every sitz bath. I gladly shared the tub with other patients on the obstetrical floor.

We didn't have a car seat for the baby. No one did back then. I held her on the drive home sitting on a donut cushion

My labor and delivery experience let me know what it was like to be helpless and not in control. I was at the mercy of the doctor and nurses. It also gave me a new awareness of empathy.

Chapter Eight

OB SUPERVISOR
1979-1983

To my surprise, while on maternity leave, the Director of Nursing called to offer me the OB supervisor position and I accepted the job. After having been gone for six weeks, I returned to a seven on seven off daytime shift. The unit was staffed with one LPN and one nurse's aide for each shift. I worked the opposite week of the day LPN, having the same duties as she did. With the new job came new responsibilities that included staffing, orientation of new employees, and writing and implementing new policies and procedures. I attended monthly meetings with the Director of Nursing and other nursing supervisors. The older Obstetrician soon retired and the new OB soon established his way of doing things.

This was an exciting time in the life of our small OB unit. The California OB brought with him the knowledge of new and modern practices. The hospital purchased three new pieces of equipment for the unit, a real time ultrasound machine, an electronic fetal monitor and an Ohio infant warmer. We kept the ultrasound in the labor room mainly utilizing it to determine presentation of the baby. The obstetrician measured the biparital diameter of the head to calculate gestational age.

He also performed amniocenteses at the bedside when the need was indicated. We gathered the supplies and he did the procedure in the labor room with ultrasound guidance. The aspirated amniotic fluid was sent to the lab for an LS ratio which indicated lung maturity.

I'd never heard him tell a patient the gender of their baby. Occasionally he scanned early complicated pregnancies.

The fetal monitor graphed the fetal heart rate and uterine contractions. We learned to read the monitor tracing to determine the impact of contractions on the baby. If there were two patients laboring, we swapped the monitor every hour between patients. There were no disposable monitor belts so we washed and dried the four we had when they got soiled.

The infant warmer was mobile, but remained in the delivery room and was used for every delivery. Heat radiated from the top and it supplied its own light source. We connected a temperature probe to the baby's torso which kept the temperature constant. Drawers underneath held needed supplies for term and premature babies.

The nurses made caps for the newborns by knotting one end of stockinet. This made perfect little caps that stretched to the size of their heads. They were put on the babies immediately after delivery to minimize heat loss from their bodies.

We used a DeLee suction catheter to suction meconium from the mouth and nose of the baby once the baby's head was delivered. Meconium is the first stool of a newborn, and sometimes occurs before birth and can possibly be aspirated leading to a potential for infection. The DeLee is a disposable device with a mucus trap and two catheters extending from the top. One catheter was used for suctioning the baby and the other one went into the mouth of the doctor or nurse. The suction was produced by sucking on the catheter pulling the meconium into the trap. If the trap overflowed the meconium went into your mouth. I can remember the first time I ever saw the OB use one.

In conjunction with the Neonatal Intensive Care Unit (NICU) in the city, the OB nurses enrolled in courses in the care of the newborn including premature babies. One day we went to a veterinary clinic where we learned to intubate sedated cats. That activity was one of the objectives we had to pass to complete the class.

We went into the NICU at times and talked with the nurses discussing different problems of newborns. A team from the NICU came to our hospital and transported premature and sick newborns to the city hospital. It was always a welcomed site to see them arrive. If we had a baby in need of assistance with breathing, the OB intubated the baby while the OB nurse and respiratory therapist bagged the newborn (provided respiratory assistance). To keep these babies' blood sugars in normal range we inserted a tiny NG tube and gave them dextrose. If indicated, the nurse inserted a twenty-two or twenty-four gauge cathlon into the tiny hand or foot for the administration of intravenous fluids and immobilized it with a tongue blade and kling. At about this time Microdrips and Buretrols were available in our hospital. The Buretrol had a graduated chamber, thus limiting the amount of fluid that a baby could receive. We learned a formula—using weight—to calculate the appropriate amount of fluid to give these infants. We counted the drops; sixty drops equaled one cc or milliliter. We kept the newborns warm, hydrated, and kept their blood sugar stable. Back in those days premature babies with immature lungs were at risk of developing hyaline membrane disease or respiratory distress syndrome. Sometimes these babies did well initially, but deteriorated hours later. They were transferred to NICU immediately.

Along with the new equipment and skills came new ways of laboring and delivering mothers. The new obstetrician saw no need for the perineal shave or the soap suds enema which made our job much easier. He ordered the narcotic Nisentil intravenously for pain in the early stage of labor.

When the patient dilated three to four centimeters the mother was offered an epidural caudal anesthesia done by the obstetrician. The nurses assisted in positioning the patient on her hands and knees to facilitate placement of the catheter. The catheter was secured with tape and medications were administered by the OB every one to two hours with the anesthetic agent Nesacaine. On occasion the nurse would re-inject the Nesacaine maintaining the effect of the anesthesia.

The OB used an amnihook to rupture the bag of water. If the baby's head remained high and the OB wanted to rupture the membranes, he took an eighteen gauge needle held it between his fingers during a vaginal exam and nicked the amniotic membrane causing a slow leak instead of a gush.

Occasionally, Pitocin inductions were done; mainly when toxemia or spontaneous rupture of membranes without labor occurred. The Pitocin was infused very carefully and the patients were on the fetal monitor. We kept blue disposable chux pads under the patients changing them often and emptying their bladders with a catheter every few hours. There were women who preferred natural childbirth which we encouraged and sometimes assisted in coaching them. I always guessed the gender of the baby while the mother was in labor. Typically, if the fetal heart rate was below 135 it was a boy, if above 140 it was a girl.

The mothers were taken to the delivery room to begin pushing. Rarely did any of them deliver in the labor room. I remember it happened once when we were transporting a patient to the delivery room. She said, "I have to push!" and she pushed out an eleven pound three ounce baby boy on the stretcher. That was the biggest baby I've ever seen born.

Usually the OB and the house supervisor assisted in transferring the patient onto the delivery table because she had little control of her legs with "a caudal." A wedge was fastened to the delivery table raising the upper body of the mother to a forty-five degree angle. This position made pushing much easier and much more productive. When placed in the lithotomy position, the legs were strapped in the stirrups.

I recall the first delivery I attended with the new obstetrician; he handed me the leather wrist straps and said," I don't ever want to see these again." I threw them away.

We used a red rubber catheter to drain the bladder before pushing to facilitate the descent of the baby. Sometimes forceps were used. If the baby did well with the delivery the mother was allowed to hold her newborn immediately after the birth for bonding. Following any repair of the perineum, ice was applied to prevent swelling and reduce pain. We recovered the patient for a couple of hours and then transported her to a room where she showered as soon as the anesthesia wore off. Patients complained minimally with their stitches.

My friend and I continued to teach prenatal classes. The hospital provided a place and the use of their movie projector. The class met once a week for six weeks beginning a new class every other month. The cost was thirty dollars. Each week we discussed a new topic and always practiced breathing and relaxation techniques. I figured if they could use these techniques until they were dilated three to four centimeters, then they could get an epidural thus bypassing the need for a narcotic. The Similac formula representative attended the class and provided instruction about infant nutrition showing a movie on breast feeding and giving all the couples a case of formula. By the end of the six weeks the couples had an idea of what to expect with labor and delivery, however you don't really know what labor is until you experience it.

The couples were instructed to bring to the hospital for labor their own pillow and a bag with the following items: a tennis ball for back labor, a paper bag for hyperventilation, Chapstick, sour lollipops, socks, and snacks for the father. The class watched the movie "The Miracle of Birth" and many of the dads had never seen anything like it. Some of them didn't look. They stared at an object in the room.

After the movie, I turned the lights up and we discussed what we'd seen. Once, after the lights came on, I noticed a father-to-be that was as white as a sheet, staring, sort of unresponsive and sitting up. He looked like someone had poured a bucket of water on his head. I went over to him, called his name, touched him on the shoulder, and he fell on the floor. I thought, "Are we gonna have to call a code on him?" I ran to the ER and grabbed an ammonia ampule and stuck it under his nose. He came around, but had no recollection of what had happened.

One night one of the moms came to the class complaining of a bad headache. She was really swollen. Her lips and nose took up half of her face. After class, I took her blood pressure, which was extremely high. She went to the OB unit where the obstetrician assessed her and delivered her thirty four week baby boy via Cesarean Section. We put the newborn in one of our white glass top incubators and strapped it to a stretcher. The OB and I rode with the baby transferring him to the NICU in the city.

I taught the classes for four and a half years enjoying every minute of it. I met many young couples during this time and have remained friends with many of them.

We became a family centered childbirth unit, encouraging the interaction of family members in the birth experience and the postpartum hospital stay. Often, the lights in the delivery room were dimmed and the couple played soft music during delivery. The mother held the baby immediately after birth for bonding. If the father wanted to, he gave the baby its first bath in warm water prepared in a nursery crib in the delivery room. Our goal was to make the birth experience special and memorable. There were some fathers that opted to stay in a waiting area. The couple was allowed to have champagne to celebrate if desired.

It was very different having the fathers in the delivery room. It took some getting used to. Most of them did well. Some cried, but most were fairly quiet. I recall one that probably wished he had kept his mouth shut.

When the OB was suturing his wife's perineum this husband said, "Hey doc how about putting in a stitch for me."

The OB slowly turned and looked at him then replied," I can do that. Come over here and I will sew your left testicle to your left leg."

OUCH!

Placentas were placed in containers and stored in the unit refrigerator. They were picked up every couple of weeks and taken to a plant were they were used in the manufacture of lotion.

Breast feeding was encouraged by the OB and the nurses. Some of the mothers wanted to, but didn't know exactly how to or what to expect.

The babies were carried to the nursery initially for observation, vital signs, eye drops and a Vitamin K injection. Our unit allowed and encouraged rooming in with the mothers. Siblings visited the mother and baby after meticulous hand washing. Unless there were problems, the pediatrician, or family practitioner performed newborn physical exams during morning rounds.

Sometimes I would voice my concern over how a newborn looked. They just looked funny, like a small head, close set eyes or weird ears. The pediatrician told me they were just "funny looking kids" then he would add, "Have you seen the mama and daddy?" Well, he was right. Genetics is a powerful thing. Soon, we just called them FLKs. I have seen some of those "funny looking kids" grow up. Some grew out of it, but some didn't.

Circumcisions and PKU tests were done prior to discharge. Circumcisions were done with a Plastibell, which stayed on falling off a few days later. Some of the mothers brought belly bands to the hospital and put them on the babies when they dressed them for discharge. Most belly bands were made at home consisting of a long piece of white cloth and a large coin. The cloth went around the baby's abdomen. A quarter or half dollar was placed over the umbilicus which was held in place with the cloth. It was believed to prevent any protrusion of the belly button.

We had six postpartum beds with a shower in each room. There were some women that refused to take a shower after having a baby because their mothers and grandmothers told them not to. The patients used disposable sitz baths and heat lamps for perineal discomfort from stitches.

Baby care companies were very generous with their products and the mothers were given gift packs and formula at discharge. One of our new family practitioners had been on staff only a month when he came beaming through the nursery door announcing, "My wife and I have a baby girl!" I gave him all the gift bags and formula he could carry. Later that week he asked if I would come by their house and look at the baby's cord. I thought, "He's a doctor and his wife is a nurse." Oh well, it was a good visit and of course her cord was fine.

The Caesarean sections post-partum bilateral tubal ligations and D&Cs were done downstairs in surgery. Breech presentations received a C-section.

There was no anesthesiologist. A nurse anesthetist administered the general anesthesia and the surgeons did their own spinals. She also administered all the medications. There were two or three nurses in the operating room during a case. Sometimes two scrubbed in and one circulated. Occasionally, the hospital surgeon assisted the OB. The OB nurse was responsible for transporting the radiant warmer to surgery and receiving the newborn. At that time, scheduled C-section patients were admitted to the hospital the evening before in preparation for the next morning's surgery. Labs were drawn, an abdominal shave prep done with a disposable razor, and a Fleets enema was given. A quick ultrasound was done before the patient left the unit to assess for breech presentation.

If spinal anesthesia was used and the couple had attended

childbirth classes, the father was permitted in the operating room for the birth. Previously, Caesarean incisions were vertical on the abdomen leaving a noticeable scar. The new OB made a Pfannenstiel incision which was a horizontal cut made right above the hairline. This incision commonly known as the 'bikini cut' allows women to expose their bellies without showing a scar. I could never look at the initial cut of the incision and still can't. It makes my skin crawl. I learned in nursing school, "Once a C-section, always a C-section." That rule was etched in stone. However, if our OB had done the previous C-section and he thought that a woman could delivery vaginally he would allow them a trial of labor.

The OB decided that he should be able to do an emergency Caesarean in the delivery room if needed. We devised a plan, decided on the team members and practiced for this event hoping it would never happen. The first emergency C-section was done for a prolapsed cord on one of our own OB nurses—*Nurse Curse*. It happened on a weekend of course. The mother was blocked and actually talked to us while the team quickly got everything and everybody in their assigned places. She was so calm. It went perfectly.

On the wall in front of the nurse's station was a large board that listed the names of the OB patients, their due date or estimated date of confinement (EDC), and any pertinent information. The board was updated each month. One patient had breech twins written by her name, so we knew that she'd have a C-section when she delivered. She came in and was admitted in the early morning. The surgery team was called in. The OB could not deliver the first baby, he tried again without success. Then he reached between the babies and discovered the reason why—conjoined twins. After enlarging both incisions, he delivered the babies. They were connected from the umbilicus to the nipple line. They were transported to University Hospital in Birmingham where it was determined they shared some vital organs and could not be separated which was unfortunate. News traveled fast that conjoined twins were born in our rural hospital. The whole town was talking about it. One of the TV stations came from the city interviewing the mother and broadcasting her story on the news that night.

❧

Early one morning an OB patient came in with abdominal pain at a gestational age of around thirty-three weeks. The baby showed a fast heartbeat, or tachycardia, on the fetal monitor. The patients belly was fairly large, but there was a knot on the side of her belly which the OB assumed was a large fibroid. She'd had a known fibroid tumor and had been on bed rest, off-and-on, during her pregnancy. After observation and assessment of the patient and baby, the OB decided to deliver the baby by Caesarean. I prepared the patient for surgery and we transported her to the operating room. He began her surgery and upon opening the abdomen, the OB realized this was a live intra-abdominal pregnancy. The baby boy was assessed, stabilized, and transferred to the NICU. The placenta was attached to the colon. The general surgeon was called in to assist in this extraordinary delivery.

The knot on the side of her abdomen was the uterus, which had been displaced by the pregnancy. The baby grew inside the abdominal cavity instead of the uterus. To have a live birth in this situation was extremely rare.

Twelve years later, I saw the mother in the grocery store and she recognized me, she said, "There he is. He's twelve years old."

What a great story I'll never forget it as long as I live. What a privilege to have been a part of that birth.

Toxemia is a common complication of pregnancy characterized by hypertension, edema, and protein in the urine. The only cure for it is delivery of the baby. Occasionally, we had patients that were admitted to the hospital for close observation to recognize worsening signs and symptoms of the disease. Sometimes they were admitted because of noncompliance with doctor's orders, especially bed rest. When toxemia patients were kept in the hospital we assessed the baby with a stress test consisting of making the patient contract with Pitocin and observing the impact of contractions on the baby. We administered Magnesium Sulfate to prevent seizures.

One day, the OB's office nurse brought a patient to the labor room. Her blood pressures were so high at her office appointment that the OB would not let her drive next door to the hospital. She had some of the highest blood pressures I'd ever seen in an OB patient. She had to be delivered and was quickly readied for a C-section. The OB and I accompanied her to the operating room. We knew the baby was premature so the hospital pediatrician was in attendance for the birth and the NICU transfer team had been notified and they were on their way. The baby was tiny weighing only two pounds and eleven ounces. He was a tough little guy. We called him "Tiny Tony". He was stabilized and transported to the city. He stayed in the NICU for weeks. Soon after he was discharged home from the NICU, his mama brought him to the doctor because his scrotum was swollen. He was admitted to the Med-Surg floor. I was asked to come to his room by the nurse to help with starting an IV and inserting an NG tube. When I went in the room, I recognized the mama and there in the middle of the huge baby bed was "Tiny Tony." He was ten weeks old. I remember the doctor shining a flashlight behind his scrotum determining that his small intestines had herniated into his scrotum. This examination is known as transillumination.

The hospital surgeon was consulted and diagnosed him with a small bowel obstruction. He talked to his mama, discussing possibilities of what he might find and the risks of surgery and anesthesia. He gave her the option of transferring him to a large hospital or keeping him here for the operation. She opted to keep him here. It was night time when the nurse anesthetist and the surgery girls were called in for the emergency operation. I came in with my mother-in-law to observe. The nurses laid him on the operating room table. He was so small—only seven pounds.

With the IV medication his little body relaxed and the nurse anesthetist intubated him, maintaining his breathing throughout the operation. When everyone was ready, and before the skin incision, the surgeon and the nurses stood quietly around him looking at the small baby under the drapes. Perhaps they were silently praying or going over the surgery in their heads. The room was so quiet; the only sound was the rhythmic, "shh-shh-shh," of the small anesthesia bag being squeezed by the nurse anesthetist. Upon exploration he found an incarcerated hernia with necrotic bowel at the end of the small intestines. He removed the dead bowel and reconnected the small intestine and repaired the hernia. After the recovery period, the nurses carried him back to his mama. The surgeon came up and talked to her with a hopeful attitude, but no guarantee for his recovery. He did recover and he thrived. Once in a while she would take him by the surgeon's office so that physician could see how he was growing. The surgeon called him, "The Miracle Baby." Tiny Tony is now thirty-one years old and has two boys of his own. What an amazing surgery team. What an amazing story he has to tell his own boys.

We saw a worsening of symptoms and lab work in a twenty-five year old gravida-two para-one, who had been admitted to the hospital for close observation of elevated blood pressure and edema. It was in the wee hours of a Friday morning when the OB determined that delivery was necessary. The surgery girls were called in for the early morning delivery. We knew the baby would be premature so we carried the anticipated supplies and the warmer to the operating room for the Caesarean section. I prepared the patient for surgery and rolled her to the surgery holding room. Baby Jessica was born at 3:44 AM. The pediatrician and I received the baby girl who was immediately transferred to the NICU in the city.

During the operation the mother began having complications. She began bleeding from her incision, her IV site, her venipuncture site, Foley, and mouth. Her blood had stopped clotting. Terrifying. She had gone into disseminated intravascular coagulation, or DIC, from low platelets and a compromised liver due to the toxemia. The hospital surgeon came in to assist with this life-threatening situation. She was given about fifty pints of blood that day. The river town responded to the call for blood donations. The blood donor line extended from the lab to the outside of the hospital down the sidewalk. That night she was transported by ambulance to the Big Bear parking lot where she was put on a helicopter and flown to the University Hospital in Birmingham. The doctors and OR nurses worked all day trying to save her life. There were no other surgeons or nurses to give them a break. There was no other nurse anesthetist to give her a break. They'd done all they could to save her life. She lived only four days after her baby girl was born. This life threatening complication of toxemia is known today as HELLP syndrome. HELLP is an acronym for hemolysis, elevated lever enzymes and low platelet count.

Another complication of pregnancy we treated was premature labor. The OB ordered the new drug Ritodrine, or Yutopar, as a tocolytic to stop premature labor. It was given around the clock and worked fairly well with some patients complaining of a fast heart rate, palpations and nausea. After several years of use it was taken off the U.S. market. We administered steroid injections IM to mothers with a risk of delivering prematurely to enhance fetal lung maturity.

It was a Sunday morning when a young couple arrived to our OB unit. This was their first baby. The couple was in our childbirth class so I knew them. We were laughing and talking as she got settled into the labor bed. I grabbed the ultrasound transducer from the fetal monitor to assess the fetal heart tones, but I couldn't hear one. A sinking feeling fell over me. I kept my best face on as I left the room to call the OB. He came quickly and with the ultrasound he confirmed our worst fears. As the patient continued in labor the OB broke her water. It was thick and green with meconium, an obvious sign of fetal distress. The full-term stillborn baby girl was delivered without any obvious reason for the demise. She looked perfect. Those are so hard, so sad.

The California OB opened his practice in the fall of 1978. He made big sacrifices to maintain his solo practice. He was always close by, either at the office next door or at home only a mile away. I can remember one year he never took a vacation. If he did he would have had to get coverage from another OB or send his patients to one in the city. He was very easy to work with and he taught me a lot. At times, he played the role of the anesthesiologist administering regional blocks to his patients and the neonatologist initiating the care of a high risk newborn.

He was very particular about his car, a Ferrari. The whole town knew about his Ferrari, a popular topic of conversation at gatherings and at dinner tables. It had a special parking place in the hospital parking lot and nobody parked next to it. Sometimes he covered it and we all thought that pretty strange, but it was probably the norm where he came from. Once I'd taken a multipara patient to the delivery room knowing she was laboring fast. The OB was on his way. I knew he'd arrive soon, but the time was *now*. I delivered the head, but the cord was so tight around the neck I couldn't get her out. I had to clamp, cut, and unwind the cord to deliver her. Everything turned out well and she named the baby, Camille. Where was the OB, who *always* made it for delivery? Someone had gotten his parking spot.

Another day stands out in my memory. It was busy enough for one labor nurse with two laboring patients. Nevertheless, a third one came up. We admitted her to a stretcher in the hallway, then a fourth, and a fifth. There were two in the labor rooms, one in the hallway and two in the second delivery room that was rarely used. I stayed after my shift with the three-to-eleven nurse and the house supervisor. We transferred the fetal monitor from patient-to-patient. The OB was inserting caudals and maintaining the blocks. The nurses were moving quickly taking vital signs, assessing contractions and fetal heart tones. We kept the chart record at the bedside. Luckily they delivered one at a time.

In the midst of this laboring frenzy, the Emergency Room called asking for a nurse to come down and evaluate a young woman with complaints of abdominal pain and constipation. The ER nurse thought she might be in labor. I answered the call and went down to the ER and found the high school girl squatting on the floor, screaming. Then her water broke. Now we all knew what her problem was. Nothing like a delivery in the ER to get everybody moving. We assisted her up onto the stretcher to check her progress. The baby's head was crowning! Between the screams and contractions, she denied being pregnant and her mother was in shock. The new hospital internal medicine doctor who was on call for the ER, came in to deliver the baby. As the doctor and I stood there wearing our sterile gloves waiting on one more push, the OB walked through the door at just the right moment and delivered the baby. She was known as "a walk in." These patients usually show up in the Emergency Room with no history of prenatal care.

The OB's practice grew and the mothers had good things to say about our unit. We offered almost anything a patient could want including caudal anesthesia and rooming in. All of us were so proud and worked hard to make our unit a success. It was a great asset to the hospital and our small community. I was devastated when our OB unit closed in April of 1983. I lost my position and was eight months pregnant looking forward to having my baby in our hospital with my hospital family. The OB moved his practice to the city and most of his patients including me went with him.

I delivered my second baby at a hospital in the city on May 31st. This experience was so much better than my first. My OB was never hurried. I got my caudle block at four centimeters dilation. He broke my water when I was on the delivery table. I was allowed to push. He cut a small episiotomy. I easily delivered my baby girl weighing eight pounds and eleven ounces. I held her as soon as she was born. She was beautiful. She nursed like a champ. I delivered on Tuesday and on Friday I was driving around town running errands. What a difference a great OB makes.

I was fortunate to get a twelve-week maternity leave because the hospital offered a voluntary layoff during summertime low-census. I drew unemployment compensation during the second six weeks of my leave and returned to work on the three-to-eleven shift as charge nurse on the Medical-Surgical floor in September.

Chapter Nine

CHARGE NURSE, MEDICAL-SURGICAL NURSING 1983-1991

With the closing of the obstetrics unit, the OB nurses and aides had no choice, but to fill vacant positions within the hospital or find jobs elsewhere. My only option was charge nurse on the familiar Medical-Surgical floor working the three-to-eleven shift which offered more memorable experiences.

My time on the evening shift was very brief and there are only two things that stand out in my memory. The hospital allowed me to leave around 5:30 PM for my supper break to go home and breast feed my three-month-old. When I returned home around 11:20 PM she was awaiting her night time feeding. She was rarely sick which I attribute to all the hospital germs I brought home to her, building her immune system.

About this time, the hospital purchased time clocks and mounted them near the nurse's station. We punched in fifteen minutes prior to the hour our shift started and punched out fifteen minutes after the hour that our shift was over. We stood in line waiting for the exact minute to punch.

Only once in my career have I ever witnessed anaphylaxis and death due to a drug reaction. The middle-aged man with a diagnosis of pneumonia had received an IM dose of Penicillin around 7 PM.

Within minutes he began having trouble breathing which advanced into full respiratory and cardiac arrest. We coded him, but couldn't bring him back. By 7:30 PM he was gone. He had no known drug allergy to Penicillin. Seeing something like that makes you mindful of administering drugs, especially antibiotics. The nurse who had given the injection was very upset of course. There was no error, it just happened.

I returned to the day shift as charge on the Medical-Surgical floor with many of the same staff working the seven-days-on, seven-days-off schedule. The older LPN had retired, but the other one was still there. I had the same duties as before with the exception of mixing piggybacks and IV fluids. The hospital purchased a Laminar Flow Hood in 1982 for the hospital pharmacy. This is a hood that flows air away from the work area where intravenous fluids are mixed allowing the pharmacist to work in an aseptic field. All the piggybacks and intravenous fluids were mixed in the pharmacy relieving us of that responsibility. I still administered the IV push medications. The east wing nurse and I were on the Code Ten Team. Whenever we heard the overhead page we took off running to the nearest stairwell. The two of us joined the rest of the Code Ten Team to perform our duties in the event of a cardiac arrest. Her duty was chest compressions and mine was the recorder. The recorder documents every intervention and every medication given during a code making sure the correct time of each action is recorded. The doctor or respiratory therapist intubated the patient and the respiratory therapist managed ventilations. The house supervisor administered the drugs. If a pharmacist was in house they responded as well.

The number of surgery patients was directly related to the hospital surgeon's work load and the increase in doctors. I still pushed that dressing cart following him into each room. My four-year-old nicknamed him "the operator". She and I were in the grocery store one day. And as children do, she ran ahead of me onto the next aisle. As I rounded the aisle, I met her running back towards me with wide eyes. I saw the surgeon midway down the aisle." She said in a scared little voice, "Mama, it's the operator!" Since that encounter, that's what I call him to this day.

There were three more hospital physicians who had been hired since I'd worked the Med-Surg floor previously. One thing they had in common; they were all older than me. Doctors are just supposed to be older—*aren't they?*

A third family medicine doctor arrived in 1981. He'd built a strong practice by the fall of '83 which added another doctor to morning rounds. He always rounded with a TAB in his hand. A TAB is a Coca-Cola drink.

A podiatrist came to our hospital in 1982. I'd never even heard the word podiatrist until he came on board. He quickly grew his practice managing the care of patients with foot problems. I met him when his child was born. He consulted on many of the admitted patients, especially diabetics, and performed foot surgeries. Some of his surgery patients returned to the floor with all kinds of hardware protruding from their feet and toes. It looked so painful. They did amazingly well and had minimal pain. He did his own dressing changes and most of his wound care. He was "low maintenance." His post-op patients wore a special shoe—sometimes for weeks. I could always spot one of his patients in town by those ugly shoes. He was never without his "black bag" full of all his podiatry stuff.

Our first internal medicine doctor came on staff in 1980. He was very smart and soft spoken. He had his own office patients and also consulted with hospital patients. He showed up at different times of the day for consults and rounds. I learned to assist him with thoracentesis, paracentesis, and bone marrow aspirations. We had disposable trays for these procedures. I prepared the patients, set up the sterile trays and assisted him with the procedure. He ordered many new and different diagnostic tests and labs which I quickly became very familiar with. Soon after he came, he began doing cardiac stress tests and Holter monitor interpretations. Patients could receive these tests at our hospital instead of going out to town to have them done. During this time our hospital installed telemetry monitoring. He did much of his work in the intensive care unit. The words *Swan-Ganz Catheter* became a common word around the ICU as the new doctor placed them and the nurses managed them. We nurses soon learned new procedures and became comfortable with his orders.

Another unforgettable patient was a man who contracted "lockjaw' or tetanus due to a farming injury. Tetanus is caused by a bacteria and can be fatal. The podiatrist was seeing him due to his wound and noticed the rigidity of his muscles. He called the internal medicine doctor to evaluate him. The muscles in his back were so rigid that they caused his body to arch backwards. The diagnosis was made and he was transferred to ICU where he was intubated and put on a ventilator. He remained on the vent for several weeks. We were all interested in the patient and his illness and kept up with him on a daily basis. Privacy laws (HIPPA) had yet to come into existence back then so we'd just ask the ICU nurses about him. After a lengthy two month hospital stay, the patient recovered and was able to go home.

The hospital opened its doors to visiting doctors who were specialists. They came from out of town for consults and surgeries. They set up offices to see and treat the people in town and surrounding areas. Some of the specialty practices had a different doctor come each week. We were accustomed to "our doctors" so this was new to us. We had to get used to these doctors and the way they liked to do things. It was good having these specialists come to our hospital and allowed the townspeople to be seen closer to home instead of traveling to a larger city for exams and procedures. It also increased revenue for the hospital. Eventually, we became comfortable with the visiting doctors and rarely encountered problems with any of them or with their patients.

Tuesday was urology day. Our visiting urologist was from India. He was the first foreign physician I'd ever worked with. He had a very heavy accent. I was used to English and Southern English, at that, so understanding him presented quite a challenge. I had to look at him when he spoke, concentrating carefully on each word. Our phone conversations were an even greater task. I had to have complete silence at the desk when speaking with him and all of my staff knew it. He operated every Tuesday morning, sending up a TURP every couple of hours. A TURP is a transurethral resection of the prostate. This surgery is performed to treat benign enlargement of the prostate. I think he fixed everybody's prostate in town. The east end nurse and I maintained the Murphy drips all day, making sure the big irrigant bags did not run dry. If that happened, we had to aspirate blood clots from the three-way Foley catheter until it was patent again. It was a must to keep the irrigation flowing. He taught us how to care for his surgical patients and came any time we called.

One Sunday morning in particular, the three-way Foley catheter of one of his surgery patients was clogged with blood clots and I couldn't get it flushed so I called the doctor. As soon as he stepped off of the elevator I could tell he was sick. He was pale and weak eyed. He was struggling with a fever. He had the flu. I told him in my best bossy charge nurse voice "You can't go in his room and you need to be at home in the bed."

He stood at the door and walked me through the steps to remedy the problem. He practiced alone so he had no partners that could answer our calls for him.

One day he called for a set of filiforms and followers. *What's he saying?* He repeated it two or three times and I still didn't know what he was talking about. He called the central sterile department asking for them and a sterile pack was brought up to the floor. He took it to the bedside of a man with a urethral stricture that needed some sort of dilation so that a Foley catheter could be inserted. The urologist opened the sterile package. The contents looked like a bunch of worms all lying next to one another. After putting on sterile gloves and lubricating the strange looking instruments with K-Y jelly, he took the filiforms and inserted them into the man's urethra then connected the followers onto the filiforms. He gradually increased the size of the dilators. I had never seen anything like this procedure before. It appeared painful for the patient. Afterwards a Foley catheter could be passed, relieving the patient's distended bladder. The patient's eyes were big as saucers and I'm sure mine were too.

A vascular-thoracic surgeon was consulted on a female patient who happened to be one hundred years old. He diagnosed her abdominal pain as a dissecting aortic aneurysm. He immediately made arrangements to transfer her to the city for surgery. I thought, "He's gonna operate on her, she's a hundred years old."

We readied her for transfer and prepared her records. I wished her well as she left our hospital by ambulance, but thinking, "If they hit the railroad tracks too hard that aneurysm might burst." Our hometown centurion survived her surgery. In the years after her surgery, she was admitted to our hospital and I got to see her again. I opened our local paper one day and there was a picture of her celebrating her 105th birthday.

After the California OB-GYN left, gynecologists came from

the city for gynecological consults. They performed their examinations in a treatment room across from the nurse's station. In this room, there was an exam table with stirrups, a mayo stand, a gooseneck lamp, and a rolling stool.

One day, I brought an elderly female patient into the exam room and assisted her onto the exam table positioning her legs in the stirrups. The gynecologist did a pelvic exam on her. After some tugging he pulled out this round object that he dropped on the mayo making a loud clang. *What was this disgusting thing he had pulled out of her?* I had no idea; it was a *pessary*. I'd never heard the word *pessary*. I found myself wondering how many years it had been in there.

The visiting ear, nose, and throat doctors were able to perform some surgeries here. Most of these were the placement of ear tubes and the removal of tonsils and adenoids.

A few days after a tonsillectomy, a young women was admitted with hemorrhaging. She came to the floor in a wheelchair leaning over a bath basin while blood poured from her mouth. I quickly started her IV and completed a quick assessment of her before calling report to her ENT. Her pulse was rapid and her blood pressure was dropping. She was anxious and scared. I called the doctor reporting her condition and her vital signs. He said to me, "Tell her to come to my office."

I repeated the report, but he was insistent upon her coming to his office. I thought, "Did he not understand me?" We put her on an ambulance and transferred her to a city hospital to have the bleeding treated and the wound repaired. When I see her in passing, she always laughs about her scary experience and thanks me for my nursing care.

From time to time, over my forty years as a nurse, I've occasionally been snapped at, yelled at, and had my feelings hurt by doctors. Usually they were tired, had a bad day, or were in the middle of some kind of emergency. But never have I ever been spoken to by anyone the way a visiting doctor spoke to me in front of my staff one day.

The doctor had scheduled a morning surgery for an older man with a history of COPD. The night nurse had reported that the man was experiencing breathing difficulty. Immediately after report I went in to check on the patient. I found him sitting up in bed with his elbows propped on the over bed table struggling to breathe. After alleviating his shortness of breath with a breathing treatment, the man still couldn't lie back in his bed. I began trying to reach the doctor, to tell him his patient was unable to have surgery this morning. I called every number that was written by his name at my nurse's station, in the ER, *and* in surgery. I could not get in touch with him. He stepped off of the elevator and walked up to the nurse's station and I began telling him about his patient and explained how I'd tried to get in touch with him. He went into a rant, yelling at me as he paced in front of the nurse's station. He went on and on. I was totally shocked by the way he acted. He said, "Lady, I pay big money for people to know where I am!" as he stomped off the floor.

One of "our doctors" happened to be standing at the desk and heard the whole outrage. He said to me, "Well, Camille, are you going to report this to the administrator or do you want me to?"

I answered, "Would you please tell him?" I never saw that doctor in our hospital again.

With our new doctors and the visiting specialists came new diagnostic tests and equipment. In 1981, our hospital opened a nuclear medicine department. We began offering diagnostic ultrasounds, as well. This new testing and technology brought new employees to our hospital. We were growing and adapting to the changes in healthcare.

In 1985, every hospital in the country went under the reimbursement system known as DRGs or diagnosis-related group. Our hospital was no exception. It was mandated by the federal government to replace the cost-based reimbursement system that had been used for years prior. We all knew it was coming and our hospital administration prepared for it.

In the years before DRG's people were admitted for just about anything and the LOS or Length of Stay would last for days. I've been present when the doctor was about to discharge "mama or daddy" when the family asked if they could stay longer so the care givers could go to the beach for the weekend. Most of the time, these requests were granted. Thinking back, some of our patients would be in the hospital for Thanksgiving and Christmas so they weren't alone for the holidays. During the blistering heat of the Southern summer, I think some patients went to the doctor with the intention of being admitted just so they would be in the air-conditioning. I think others just wanted to lie on clean sheets.

I recall an older gentleman who was admitted now and then for tests. Sometimes he would stay in his room, but when the cafeteria was open, he could be found eating there wearing a suit and tie with his suitcase at his side.

Another memorable patient was frequently admitted with arthritic knees. She kept a can of WD-40 at her bedside and kept her knees greased with the lubricant. She swore by it. The nurses labeled some of the patients as "comers-and-goers" and "comers-and-stayers." The "comers-and-stayers" had a new ailment every time the doctor was ready to discharge them. With the advent of DRGs these less than legitimate patient admissions and hospital stays were over. These were hard times for our hospital and many others, but we weathered the changes. Now, when patients are admitted they're sicker and have much shorter hospital stays.

In 1987, a neighboring hospital closed its doors, thus bringing us more patients and some of its doctors, as well. There were now more doctors to round with including another general surgeon. We quickly learned his orders and how he wanted things done. He dressed very professionally, always wearing a crisp, clean lab coat. He did a lot of wound care especially on bed bound patients. One day, he and I were doing a wound debridement on a decubitus hip ulcer and part of the femur bone came off in my hand. I've seen some bad decubitus ulcers in my day and this *was* one of the worst.

The family practice doctors had offices in the nearby town, but admitted patients to our hospital, thus allowing patients to keep their own doctors.

One of the general practice doctors that came brought many new patients to our hospital. After working with him awhile, I heard that he could conjure warts off people. Well, I had the opportunity to tell him about my ten-year-old daughter who had a huge wart on her knee and she wouldn't let me take her to have it removed. He told me to bring her to the hospital on his call night and he would "talk it off." I brought her, and he placed his hands around her knee speaking some words I'd never heard. Two weeks later she had a wreck on her bicycle, skinning her knee on the blacktop. Well, the wart *was* gone.

An anesthesiologist also came to our hospital with this group of doctors. She was the first anesthesiologist at our hospital and the first female doctor I'd ever worked with. The nurse anesthetists finally had a doctor to work with them. Prior to her coming, the nurse anesthetists worked under the orders of the surgeon.

During this same time period, two new family practice doctors came to town. They set up their practice in the office building next to the hospital. Two new internal medicine doctors also came on staff. All four of these doctors were younger than I was and I was only thirty-two. It was strange to be working with doctors younger than I. *So, would I act any differently around these young doctors?* No. I was always respectful and always answered them with "Yes, Sir," and "No, Sir".

I'd known one of the young internal medicine doctors for a few years. He was a younger brother to the hospital's first internal medicine doctor. He was really fun to work with. He popularized the expression "low sick" and the nurses soon adopted the term to categorize the status of a critical patient. Some of the young docs brought their children with them when they came in to round mainly on the weekend. This was new to us. Some would sit at the nurse's station very quietly while others were into everything. It was usually the unit clerk that took on the babysitting duties.

By the end of the eighties we had quite a number of doctors on staff, either our own or visiting ones. As nurses do, we adapted to new doctors and their orders. We were constantly learning. Now the metal tape dispenser was full of different colored rolls of tape. We had so many doctors on staff that we even had to add striped colored tape to identify them.

Some days I felt like I was working on a pediatric unit. We admitted children of all ages, with more of them being admitted during the winter months due to seasonal illnesses. I could walk down the west end of the floor and tell which room they were in simply by hearing their barking coughs. They barked like seals. They were under croup tents which respiratory therapy managed, releasing the nursing staff of that responsibility.

We no longer used Aspirin for fever because of Reye's Syndrome, a potentially fatal illness. Instead, we gave Tylenol. I started more IVs on children than before primarily because the most recent family practice doctors ordered IV fluids on their pediatric patients with IV antibiotics for infection. I used a papoose board to restrain them. It sounds sort of mean, but a still target is easier to hit than a moving one. The three papoose boards were kept in the ER. They were sized differently. I placed the IV in their hands or feet, usually with one stick. I always used an arm board to keep the extremity immobile and wrapped it with lots of gauze dressing. Of course, this was very traumatic for the child and parents. I told the parents that they could leave the room or stay and hold a hand if they wanted to. Having the parents stand over me watching really didn't bother me.

Most of the medicines ordered for these little guys were in liquid form. We didn't use syringes to give their medicines, but poured it into their mouths with a medicine cup. Often they would spit it out as soon as it was given. At the end of the day, the front of our uniforms would be splattered with failed attempts at the administration of those sticky oral medications.

Toddlers were always sticking things where they didn't belong. There was a three-year-old in particular that stuck a fat butterbean in his ear. His doctor tried to get it out with some small forceps and could not grab it. One morning I decided that I was going to get it. I went into his room determined to get it out, but he was more determined that I would not. He was wiggling around screaming and crying. His mama and I tried to hold him still. I couldn't get a hold on that butterbean. He won that battle. After three or four days of being in the hospital an ENT came and finally removed it. It was starting to sprout.

There were two boys in and out of the hospital with sickle cell anemia. It's a terrible genetic disease causing severe pain and denying its victims normal lives. They were small boys when I first met them. They grew into teenagers during my years of Med-Surg nursing. It was hard to watch them suffer with each admission. We gave them narcotics for pain. Because these poor children had endured so many previous IVs, they were very difficult to start IVs on and we were forced to stick them several times before a patent intravenous line could be established. One of them lived to adulthood; the other did not.

One of my favorite patients was a little girl with Cerebral Palsy. She was born in 1968 at twenty-seven weeks gestation when her mother's water broke. What a miracle that she survived and is now forty-five years old. She was admitted to the hospital

93

occasionally. She was a brave little girl and always seemed happy. There's no telling how many miles her parents and sisters have pushed her in her wheelchair. I saw her a few years ago at a wedding. I squatted down in front of her wheelchair and talked to her. I asked her if she remembered me and she replied in her giggly voice, "Ponytail."

The hospital surgeons saw their share of pediatric patients, usually as consults. An appendectomy was the most common operation that they performed on children. These patients usually did well and were discharged sooner than adults.

They performed operations on infants too. Pyloric stenosis is a congenital defect causing a narrowing of the stomach into the small intestines. It causes projectile vomiting and is commonly diagnosed within the first few weeks of life. These babies, most often first born males, exhibited failure to thrive. A small vertical incision was made above the umbilicus releasing the tight muscle causing the problem. This operation fixed the problem immediately. One of these babies lived next door to me. His scar was quite visible in the summer when he played outdoors without his shirt on, reminding me of his operation when he was only six weeks old.

It was a Sunday afternoon in the late eighties when a beautiful little redhead was admitted to our floor in DKA. DKA is Diabetic Ketoacidosis, and can be the first sign of undiagnosed diabetes. The little girl was five years old. Her mother was worried, crying at the bedside, holding her hand and rubbing her face. Her pale skin showed mottling in her extremities. Her breathing was very erratic. She was very sick. I stayed at her bedside monitoring her closely. One of the young internal medicine docs was covering the ER. He admitted her and continued her care on the floor. He too was very concerned and stayed close by as he treated the patient explaining the child's critical condition to the mother. He had a difficult time finding an accepting doctor and facility for transfer. Finally, a pediatrician accepted the child. I'd not heard of the pediatrician, but knew of the hospital. Our team worked quickly to ready the patient and her records for transfer. I heard weeks later that the little girl was doing well, but I never saw her again.

Fast forward to 2004. I was sitting in a pediatrician's office with my granddaughter and it occurred to me that this was the name of the pediatrician that accepted the transfer of the little five year old so many years ago. After checking my grandchild in, I asked him if he remembered the little redhead named Amelia—not her real name—that was transferred to him in the late eighties with DKA. He replied, "Yes, I do. She's twenty-seven now and is still my patient."

I saw many medical advances during my time on the medical-surgical floor. The first laparoscopic cholecystectomy (gallbladder removal) was done at our hospital in 1991 by one of the visiting surgeons. It was amazing how well these patients did. Most of them stayed overnight and were discharged the next morning. They were eating and up moving around a few hours after the surgery. This was a tremendous difference from the open cholecystectomies. Occasionally, an open surgery was necessary when there were complications with the gall bladder such as an infection.

We were fortunate to have our own gynecologist at the hospital in the late eighties. He did many of his GYN surgeries laparoscopically. The recovery room nurses applied an estrogen patch to some of his patients who had undergone hysterectomies. Upon discharge, the gynecologist gave instructions to, "Change the patch before church on Sunday and after prayer meeting on Wednesday night," as he handed them the prescription.

One of the biggest impacts on our hospital during the eighties was the advancement of gastrointestinal ulcer therapy. Before the days of Tagamet and Zantac, ulcer patients were treated with a diet of half and half alternating with Mylanta. Every two hours the nurses gave one or the other around the clock. If the ulcer was bleeding or if the patient had recurrent ulcers, surgery was required to remove the ulcerated part of the stomach and cut the vagus nerve to decrease the production of acid. These patients could be very sick. Abusers of alcohol were prone to the development of this condition and were admitted frequently for treatment. This was the case with a young man that had been admitted with sever ulcer disease.

The "Operator" had studied his chart and was aware of his history before he went in to evaluate him. I accompanied him into the room. The man was lying there with a nasogastric tube connected to suction, receiving IV fluids, and obviously in much pain. He was very weak.

The "Operator" stood there looking at him and finally spoke in his loud voice, "B-O-Y ...Pull this shit again, don't call me, call the funeral home!"

Did he really just say that to this man? One thing was for sure, the "Operator" never sugar coated anything.

In the late eighties doctors learned that most ulcers were caused by a bacteria known as Helicobacter pylori, or H pylori, and began treating them with medications decreasing gastric acid and thus, the need for the gastric surgery. The first internal medicine doctor began doing endoscopies of the upper GI tract, diagnosing and treating ulcers along with other upper GI problems. The GI lab was located in the recovery room. He worked with the surgical nurses to perform endoscopic procedures. He left for a couple of years to do a fellowship in gastrointestinal medicine and, upon completion, returned to our hospital as a gastroenterologist.

The hospital remodeled what was formerly the obstetrical unit, opening a new and spacious GI lab in 1990. One of the most common procedures done was a colonoscopy. The endoscopes used in these procedures were like the laparoscope. There was an eye piece the doctor looked through instead of a camera like these scopes currently have. The eye piece was connected to the scope, putting the doctor in close proximity of the patient. He always wore a disposable gown and goggles to protect himself. There were a few weeks just after the GI lab opened when there was no regular GI nurse to administer the intravenous sedation of mainly Demerol and Versed. I was one of the registered nurses that had been trained in giving the conscious sedation, so I worked in the lab sometimes on my days off. One day, as I was administering sedation to a patient having a colonoscopy the gastroenterologist said to me, "Camille, I want you to learn how to assist me in doing biopsies, just in case I need you to help me sometime."

I thought, *I really like it on this end of the patient sitting here on my stool pushing a little medicine and watching them breathe.*

I replied, "I'm fine, but I really don't want to learn how to do that."

After a little coaxing I reluctantly agreed and took my position at the other end of the patient. He gave me instructions on how to, grasp the tissue and pull the wire out with the tissue in the tiny forceps. I was pulling the wire out of the scope so fast it came out and flicked colon contents all over his goggles. It was so funny, I tried not to laugh, but he never asked me to help him with a biopsy ever again.

Through endoscopy—instead of open surgery—the doctor was able to insert a PEG tube into the stomach usually for feeding and the administration of medicines. PEG tubes were much more comfortable for patients and were easier to maintain than the nasogastric or the old gastrostomy feeding tubes. The gastroenterologist offered much to our town and surrounding area in the diagnosis and treatment of various gastrointestinal ailments. He remains the hospital gastroenterologist today.

I witnessed advancements in intravenous therapy during the eighties. Most all of our patients had an IV pump to administer their fluids and piggybacks. A frequent order was an IV fluid to run KVO; we did that before the use of Heparin locks. Most cancer patients had some kind of port through which to administer chemotherapy and fluids. I learned how to manage these ports. Some RNs became certified in the administration of chemotherapy. If labs were ordered on these patients the RN drew the blood from the ports and flushed them with either Heparin, a blood thinner or normal saline. Some patients, who were unable to absorb nutrition by eating or with a tube feeding, received total parenteral nutrition or TPN. This is a mixture of amino acids, lipids, vitamins, glucose and other dietary minerals the body needs to live. The lipids were white. It was strange to see that run into a vein.

In a nearby city, cardiac surgeons were performing open heart surgeries on patients to bypass clogged arteries of the heart. My daddy was one of these patients undergoing surgery for five bypass grafts in 1982. It was an eleven day hospitalization with a tough road of recovery. His graphs lasted eighteen years before any reoccurrence of heart problems. That surgery afforded him a good and active life until he was eighty-seven years old. He was never short of breath and never wore oxygen.

≈∽

Emphysema patients were readmitted time after time. I talked to them about consequences of smoking. They usually agreed with me. Sometimes I saw them around town and of course, they were still smoking. Occasionally, they avoided me. It was only a matter of time before they were back in the hospital suffering from another exacerbation of COPD (Chronic Obstructive Pulmonary Disease).

As a nurse, I paid particular attention to anything on the news or in magazines about AIDS. AIDS was scary and the medical world knew little about the illness. It brought up an awareness in me that I hadn't had before.

I remember well, the first known AIDS patient that was admitted to our floor. I don't recall how he contracted the illness. He was an angry young man, belligerent and hard to control at times. He spit on one of our nurses. Once, I had to give him an intramuscular injection to calm him down. It took the nurses, nurse's aides and an orderly to hold him so that I could administer the medication. I was nervous as I entered his room. I made sure he was well restrained, gave the injection, and quickly backed away from him. As a nurse, you can't pick your patients and he was a difficult one.

There was also Hepatitis B and C looming out there. The nurses were given a series of injections to protect us from Hepatitis B. I began wearing surgical gloves to start IVs. The gloves had to be worn tightly in order for me to feel the veins. Certainly no glove will prevent a needle stick, but they keep blood off your hands. Soon there were disposable gloves supplied in each patient's room. The nurses and nurse's aides were instructed to wear them in the presence of any body fluids and wound care. It was an adjustment, but we used them. The hospital also mounted sharps containers on the walls in patient rooms for needles and scalpel blades. Gone was the unsafe IV tray that we had all used. It was a different world with new diseases, many without cures.

కింఈ

In the early eighties terminally ill patients, especially cancer patients were given Bromptom's cocktail for pain. It was an elixir containing morphine, cocaine and ethyl alcohol. The patient kept it at the bedside. PCA, or patient controlled analgesia pumps, were used for pain management during the late eighties. With surgery patients, the pain pumps were set up in the recovery room and brought to the floor with the patients. They were effective. Sometimes I set them up for admitted patients experiencing severe pain. There were always two registered nurses that programmed the pump. We observed the patients closely for symptoms of respiratory depression. There may have been an oxygen saturation monitor in surgery and the intensive care unit, but certainly not on the floor. We kept a close watch on their respirations. As the eighties progressed more IV pain medications were used for pain management. For instance, kidney stone patients who previously received IM pain medication were later given IV Morphine.

I remember when we started administering Toradol. It was the podiatrist who introduced this good medicine. We still use it today with our C-sections.

We nursed our share of dying patients. Sometimes these patients clung to life for days and we thought their next breath would be their last. Sometimes they rallied a bit. The nurses had a saying for this phenomenon; "They are getting better to die." Too many times than I care to admit, I've heard "the death rattle." I knew it wouldn't be long after that started. It often seemed that death came in threes. If there were two deaths on the floor, we knew there were be a third not far behind. There were patients that would beg for a cigarette on their death bed. Yes, I've cut their oxygen off, lit one, and let them take a few drags. It's sad that someone's last request is a puff on a cigarette. We tried to keep them as comfortable as possible, keeping them clean and repositioned frequently. I was taught that hearing was the last of the senses to go, so we were always mindful of things we said around the dying. The patients that were allowed to die without any sort of resuscitation had what was known as a "No Code" ordered. Years later that order was changed to DNR, or Do Not Resuscitate.

As the eighties progressed there was more and more paperwork, of course. In those days it was an effort to transfer a patient back to the nursing home. I had to call the Director of Nursing and give a detailed report to her then complete a nursing home transfer form. There was additional paperwork involved in admitting and discharging patients.

I recall new equipment that was purchased for patient use. Glucometers, T-pumps, and electronic thermometers. Those thermometers were a great invention, especially with pediatric patients. We mainly used a T-pump on patients with muscle pain and thrombophlebitis. We began using TED hose on some of the bedbound patients.

Seems like I gave many TB skin test in the eighties. The order read PPD with mumps control. I gave an intradermal injection in each forearm. They were read three days later.

We had our share of memorable patients. I've told the stories of quite a few, but none are as memorable as one tall, heavyset lady who leaned over the nurse's station counter demanding that we discharge her immediately. The hospital gown was way too short for her, but that hardly mattered since the back was left untied, exposing all of her rather large backside. Upon explaining that her discharge would take a few minutes she grabbed up the *WET FLOOR* sign and began swinging it at the nurses. Help arrived quickly. Finally, she was talked into going back to her room, but she was agitated and defiant. Her attending doctor was called and came immediately. She knew him of course and allowed him to come to her bedside. He spoke softly trying to calm her down. Just when the doctor thought he was making some headway, she suddenly grabbed him holding him in a headlock. The orderlies and the hospital physical therapist had to man handle her to free the doctor. Arrangements were made and she was transferred to one of the state mental hospitals that day.

❦

Although her swallowing had been inhibited by a previous stroke, the frail elderly woman was still able to speak well enough to communicate. She had a feeding tube that was connected to a feeding pump allowing her to receive feeding continuously. She told the nurses that there was a little mouse in her room. No one had seen a mouse and we thought she was confused. During rounds one night, the evening nurse entered her room quietly and saw a small mouse standing on her feeding pump sucking the Ensure out of the tubing. Of course the nurse saved the tubing to show us the tiny hole made by the mouse.

❦

The town newspaper was published every Wednesday and could be purchased for a quarter. Every week there was a list of the hospital patients. Patients were given the option whether or not they wanted their names listed. This went on for years. I guess the HIPPA mandate ended that.

The hospital published a newsletter every quarter beginning in 1979 spotlighting different employees, doctors and departments. It was a great little paper including pictures of new employees, awards, Christmas lunches and the hospital picnics. Of course, I saved my copies and still have them.

⇝⇜

If there was ever any sort of disaster or multiple victims coming in to the emergency room, off duty nurses were called in. I recall hearing sirens scream one afternoon while my girls and I were at an Easter egg hunt at our church. I knew that something bad had happened. Upon returning home, the hospital called asking me to come in to help in the emergency room with a bad car accident involving multiple victims. I quickly got a babysitter and reported to the ER. Even though many of us didn't work in the Emergency Room we functioned as a team taking vital signs, cleaning wounds, maintaining IVs, and assisting the doctors.

The ambulances kept bringing young men in. There were four in all. The fourth victim had to be cut from the car with the "Jaws of Life." As he rolled off the ambulance, I recognized him. It was my ex-husband.

The hospital doctors worked diligently to save them all. One of the young men did not survive. I'll never forget seeing his mama come into the waiting room and the doctor meeting her to tell her what no parent ever wants to hear. It was awful. It was a bad afternoon in the ER.

One night, I was awakened by a phone call asking me to come to the hospital in the middle of the night to help evacuate patients due to a bomb threat. I didn't recognize the voice and was at home with my two girls so I called my next door neighbor, also a R.N., to make sure the call was legitimate. It was the coldest night of the year when we evacuated the full hospital to the parking lot. Ambulances came from our town and the surrounding areas to accommodate ICU patients. The on duty and off duty employees worked together to see that the patients were cared for. We stayed in the parking lot for hours awaiting the all clear. Thankfully, it was a hoax, but an appalling one.

❧

The local folks came to our hospital not only for health care, but for other reasons. Here in Alabama especially in the springtime we have many days of bad weather, thunderstorms and tornadoes. When there was the threat of bad weather, there were several townspeople that would sit in the hospital lobby until the storm was over. Night or day they'd come, sometimes staying for hours.

It was common knowledge that our cafeteria provided really good inexpensive food. On Sunday the nurses and aides were mindful of the time because we had to beat the Baptist congregation to the cafeteria or we'd be lined up out the door taking up our allotted time for lunch. We got there between 11 and 11:30 AM to beat the crowd. It would be afternoon before the Methodist would arrive.

Not only did we work together, but we also played together. In the spring of '86 the hospital sponsored a women's softball team called "The Hotshots." The team was made up of hospital employees; mostly nurses. Some of us played backyard softball growing up and a few of us played in high school. We practiced a couple of afternoons a week after work. Most of us had kids and we brought them to practice with us. The older kids looked after the younger ones.

At our first practice, the coach, the internal medicine doctor, was hitting line drives to us. Our short stop missed one and it popped her in the head leaving a perfect imprint of the stitches of the ball on her forehead.

Most of the hospital employees knew who played softball due to our obvious injuries. Any injuries below the knee were seen by the hospital podiatrist. It seemed as though one of us was in the ER every week. We played on Monday nights in the "rec" league. I don't think we won a single game our first year, but we had a great time. Over the years, some of us continued to play and some dropped out. In time, we did improve and won some games.

The hospital hosted annual hospital picnics. These will always be a fond memory for me. They were great fun and were held in different places. Everyone looked forward to them and there was always a large turnout. The department heads were in charge of different events. Some of the employees and doctors became entertainers for the night, sharing their talents. As the years went by, the picnics were held in conjunction with National Hospital Week in May. A theme was chosen and everyone worked around that theme, utilizing props and costumes. Our management worked hard to make fun and enjoyable picnics in the parking lot of our hospital.

After fifteen years of working at the community hospital, it was time for a change. I loved my hospital family, as it was my comfort zone and it was hard to leave. I knew almost everyone that worked there. I had worked every other weekend for the past fifteen years and I wanted more scheduling flexibility with less weekends. I had talked to some of the home health nurses and the freedom that home health allowed really appealed to me. It just so happened that one of the home health agency office managers was a patient on my floor. After talking to her, I decided that I would like to try it. Soon after, I called her to apply for a job with the agency. She had an opening for a visit nurse in her office and she hired me over the phone.

Chapter Ten

HOME HEALTH NURSE
1991-2000

The summer of '91 brought many changes to my nursing career. I was eager to begin a new job with one of the largest home health agencies in the state of Alabama. I looked forward to weekends off. I traveled thirty miles to my office that managed the care of 150 patients, including patients in the area where I grew up. I looked forward to seeing some of the "old-home folks" whom I had known since childhood.

After an agency wide orientation, I settled in my new office under the direction of the nurse who hired me. I shadowed a visit nurse a few days to get a feel for providing treatment in the home. I was confident in my nursing skills, but had to adapt them to the home.

The paperwork that went with this job was overwhelming. I'd never heard the word "recert", short for recertification, which seemingly became the most important spoken word in the office. I had to learn and understand the HIM 11, the Medicare Benefit Policy Manual that governed the rules and regulations of Medicare patients. The majority of our patients were on Medicare, but we also had Medicaid, private insurance, and private pay patients, each with their own guidelines.

I received a nurse-bag stocked with these supplies: blood pressure cuff, stethoscope, glucometer, disposable gloves, sharp box for needles and syringes, alcohol preps, germicidal wipes, band aids, antimicrobial soap, paper towels, needles, syringes, heavy duty toenail clippers, and a lab box that contained supplies for drawing blood. We were issued a bathroom scale because we weighed all patients who could stand. Additionally, I was also supplied with a huge trunk box that had just about everything you might need in the care of the patients. For example, it carried dressing supplies, Foley catheters, and skin care products just to name a few. I felt like I had a mini-supply closet with me. I knew I'd *arrived* when I was issued a pager that received text messages.

Home Health nurses provided skilled patient care in patient's home as ordered by the physician. They included, but were not limited to the following:

Assessment and observation with every skilled nurse visit
Gastrostomy tube change every 6 weeks and PRN
Foley catheter change every month and PRN
Tracheotomy tube changes
Intravenous therapy and site care
Parental nutrition
Administer injections
Venipuncture
Wound care, sometimes daily or twice daily
Remove sutures or staples
Bladder irrigations
Chest physiotherapy
Ostomy care and instruction
Inhalation therapy
Digital removal of impaction with follow up enemas
Prefill insulin syringes weekly
Prefill med box weekly
Instruction of disease process
Instruction of medications
Assess response to medications
Management of tracheotomy tube
Management of Foley catheter
Management of supra pubic catheters
Management of enteral feedings

Can you imagine doing some of these things by yourself in a home? The most worrisome skill for me was changing a trach and the worst one was digital removal of impactions with enemas. What a mess that was.

With my assessment of the patient, I always did a quick check of the feet. If they couldn't take off their shoes and socks I did it for them. I looked between each toe and the rest of the foot for any new wounds. Many of our patients were diabetic or had bad circulation making them unaware of foot wounds. I've seen badly infected feet that needed immediate treatment. I've seen sewing or insulin needles stuck in their feet and they wouldn't even know it. One rule we preached was "do not walk around bare footed." Once a month I cut their toenails wearing safety goggles to prevent flying nails from getting in my eyes.

The nurses and the home health aides wore white uniforms, usually pants or split skirts with white duty shoes. Most of us wore tennis shoes. I had two pair, one pair for fair days and a pair for rainy days. I wore short sleeves year round, layering my uniforms in the winter. Most of the elderly are known for being "cold natured," so they kept their houses hot in the winter and hot in the summer. Some of them had wood heaters or fire places, and there were no thermostats. Sometimes it would be so hot it would take your breath away. *How could anybody live in that heat?* I peeled off layers as soon as I entered these hot houses.

After my orientation, I began making a few visits a day taking my time with the skills and the documentation. One of my most memorable visits was to a very rural house—you might say "cow pasture" rural. I pulled up in front of the old farmhouse on a hot humid afternoon to visit a bed-bound patient. I noticed the windows were open and there were no screens. I knocked on the door, and no one answered. So I opened the door and called the man's name. I heard him making noises, but he couldn't speak. I found him in his bed, soiled, and with flies stuck to his trach secretions. My first thought was, *"I should have stayed at the hospital!"* I didn't know where to start. In most homes the supplies are kept together in a designated place, so I located a bath basin, wash cloths, and soap. Gratefully, I found there was hot running water. I started at the top and cleaned him up. Thank Goodness for gloves and linen savers.

After a few weeks, I was assigned a "patient load". Some of

106

them I knew, and a couple of them were my teachers whom I hadn't seen in a while.

Soon I became organized and began to know the patients. I scheduled skilled nursing visits and home health aide visits around the skills to be performed and the habits of the patients. For example, if a patient needed a fasting blood sugar, I called them the night before (if they had a phone) to remind them that I would be there the next morning before breakfast. Labs were drawn, kept on ice, and dropped off at the nearest hospital or clinic lab.

I thought all old people got up early. No, some of them liked to sleep late. I quickly learned not to schedule visits during the patient or the caregiver's favorite soap opera or naptime. I called the patients from the office or from my parents' house telling them what time to expect my visit. If they had a dog, I requested they put the dog up.

By the fall I had a handle on the field work and the paperwork. I was becoming adept at scheduling and making skilled nurse visits, scheduling home health aide visits, doing recerts, updating the patient charts including care plans, doctor's orders, and drug lists.

Another job task we had was to monitor the home health care aids and periodically supervise their visits. Also, I attended patient care conferences once a week where we discussed the plan of care and the recertification of the patients. I liked the flexibility of the job, leaving my house around 6:30 AM and being back home to pick up my girls from school at 2:45 PM. Most days I put eighty to 100 miles on my Chevy Astro Van. It wasn't good on gas mileage, but it was dependable and dependable is what you need in a vehicle traveling in rural Alabama where gas stations and houses are miles apart. It was not unusual to travel on dirt roads, one lane bridges, or roads riddled with pot holes.

Once I locked my keys in my van out in the middle of nowhere. My daddy came and rescued me. From then on I had a magnetic key box with a spare key hidden under my bumper. There were many times I had to rely on the extra key during my home nursing years. I utilized one of the old bag phones that may or may not have worked away from town. This vintage phone was housed in a bag that I placed on the dashboard of my van. A cord connected the handset to the receiver.

I either carried my lunch or ate hot dogs from a convenience store. I have to admit, those hot dogs cooked on the rotisserie were mighty tasty. I was mindful of a couple of houses that served up the best hot cornbread at lunch time, and they always asked me to eat. The aroma was intoxicating.

"Yes, ma'am," I replied. "All I need is a little butter and, yes, ma'am, some sweet tea would be wonderful. "

The patient's home was always treated with respect. I adapted to their environment, no matter how bad it was, often improvising with whatever was available. Sometimes there was no hot water, so we heated it on the stove. If there was poor lighting and the patient was ambulatory, we moved them to a room with better lighting. If the patient was bed bound and needed a catheter change, we used a flashlight in those situations where lighting was inadequate. If there was no table at the bedside, we would drag in a chair from another room making an area to lay out the dressing supplies or Foley kit. As in all nursing practices, hand washing was the number one infection control measure. We washed our hands at the beginning and the end of each visit. Many homes had running water, but no soap and no paper towels. I would never dry my hands on a kitchen towel hanging on a stove or a towel hanging in the bathroom. Some homes had no indoor plumbing at all. Usually there was a spigot in the yard where water was collected in a bucket and taken into the house. These people used potty chairs for elimination and emptied the buckets in the back yard. Needless to say the backyard had a lush coat of healthy green grass.

I documented most of my nurse's notes in the home, finishing up with any orders or medicine updates in my van parked under the shade of a big oak in the summer and in the sunshine on cold days. We kept a log of the visit time and the mileage which was reimbursed at twenty-five cents per mile.

Most of the visits were fairly routine, but occasionally there might be an emergency and the nurse had to make decisions on what to do. If I called an ambulance I would, of course, wait for its arrival. Physicians were contacted to advise of any change in condition, a new wound, or obtain new orders. One big difference in home health nursing was that you were on your own. There was not another nurse to back you up, provide a second opinion, or perform a venipuncture if you were unable to do it. Of benefit was continuity of nursing care, usually with the same nurses seeing the same patients. The visiting nurse continued home health visits until the patient was discharged per MD order, if they were no longer considered homebound, goals were met, or the patient was placed in a nursing home.

Our office had an admissions nurse, but occasionally the visiting nurses did the admission and initiated care on weekends, holidays and after hours. First in the admission process was a referral from the MD. The nurse went to the home for an evaluation and assessment of the patient. She wrote the order for services on the "485" including: Skilled Nursing, Home Health Aide, Physical Therapy, Speech Therapy, Occupational Therapy, Dietitian, ET (Enterostomal Therapy) Nurse, or Social Worker.

Every patient and diagnosis was different. The physician order also included the number of visits, patient supplies, and DME or durable medical equipment. Goals were determined and written on the doctor's orders. The nurse assessed the home for safety, instructing the caregiver in ways to make the environment safer such as installing grab bars in the bathroom, widening doorways, and removing throw rugs which were a fall hazard. The nurse obtained the orders from the physician, made the necessary referrals, ordered DME supplies, such as wheelchairs, oxygen, shower chairs, etc…

She completed a home health aide instruction sheet. In every chart was a demographic sheet or directions to the patient's home. Here are typical directions on a demographic sheet:

> *"Turn right from the office onto Highway 37. Go through town past Piggly Wiggly. Take a right at the first traffic light past Piggly Wiggly onto County Road 77. Continue 8 miles until you run on to a dirt road. Slow down there is a bump. Go 2 miles on the dirt road, and you will see a white house with a porch across the front on the right side of the road. The number 4896 is on the mailbox. The patient and caregiver stay in the back of the house go to the back door. The little dog in the yard won't bite; he just barks."*

I managed the care of some wonderful patients while I worked in that office. I recall two women; both lived in beautiful homes on the lake and were actually caregivers to their husbands. They didn't know each other. An orthopedic surgeon from Georgia performed bilateral knee replacements on both women. I didn't know that was an option. Both patients said they couldn't be "out of commission" that long for each knee to be done, so the doctor did both knees at the same time. It was unbelievable how well they did. He operated on many of the people who lived in that area. I never met him, but his patients recovered exceedingly well.

One of my monthly Foley changes was done on a wheelchair bound patient whose wife was his caregiver. They lived in an old house heated with open fire places, and the wife kept the fires stoked. They had cats and kittens roaming all over the house. One day, a nurse opened their refrigerator and a cat jumped out. A jar of mayonnaise was left on the counter all the time. *Ugh. Can you do that?* You could see through the flooring to the ground in some places. While changing the man's catheter, fleas would cover my legs from the knees down. I've been there when the caregiver had gone into to town, and the patient was left alone. I would find him rolling around the house in his wheelchair, eating dry grits out of the box. They would be all over his face and spilled down the front of his clothes. It was one of the filthiest houses I visited, but it was their home and they were happy there. I made my visits there in the mornings. It never failed that his sweet wife handed me a biscuit wrapped in a paper towel to take with me. I thanked her knowing I would never eat it.

Some of the homes had roaches crawling on just about everything in the house. I've seen them perched on top of a curtain like they were watching everything I was doing. One of our patients who was bedbound/wheelchair bound had an electric alternating air mattress on her hospital bed. The pump quit working so I called the DME supplier to exchange it. The motorized pump had so many roaches in it that it jammed the motor. Our agency helped patients that had infestations in getting pest control in the home.

One winter was accompanied by a bad outbreak of the flu. Some of the elderly became very sick, requiring extra visits. If the patients got the flu, usually the caregivers would have it too. I took the flu shot and felt protected as I was exposed repeatedly that year.

After a year, I transferred to an office literally a half mile from my house. I really needed to be in the same town with my girls. It, too, was a big office with around 200 patients. I knew most of the nurses, home health aides, and office staff. Basically, I had the same job with new patients, but I entered into the call rotation. I knew many of my assigned patients and where they lived. I was hopeful there was a caregiver who cooked good cornbread in my new area.

Regarding the call rotation, we were paid a flat fee of twenty-five dollars a night for call. Weekend call began on Fridays at 4:30 PM through 8 AM Monday morning. We received $150 for weekend call. When the call nurse left the office she carried "the suitcase" with her. It held updated files on all the patients.

My most memorable call night involved a patient who had a gastrostomy feeding tube. The G-tube had fallen out, and there was a risk the stoma opening would close up if left unattended. Due to the cost of G-tubes, we did not keep them in our trunk box, so that meant a stop by the office in the middle of the night. I obtained the G-tube and drove to the mobile home where the patient lived. I prepared the patient, and inflated the bulb to check for leakage prior to insertion. Well, it wouldn't deflate. I traveled back to the office, grabbed another tube, drove back to the patient's home and inserted the tube. So from then on, I did not inflate the bulb on any tubes prior to insertion. I never did have a problem with another G-tube since that night.

My first computer challenge began in 1993 when the agency purchased the PTCT home health program. The nurses received training and were issued hand held devices that held the patient information. Information was downloaded into the handhelds the evening before or the morning of the visit prior to leaving the office. Soon we had modems, and we could download from our home phones. At the end of the day we downloaded the information to the office where it was printed and placed in hard charts. I went into the home, made the visit and entered information into the handheld as I drove to the next patient visit. I suppose it was a form of texting and driving. Surprisingly, I mastered it quickly as it facilitated the visits and paperwork.

One of the highlights of working in this office was having BSN students come as part of their home heath rotation. I loved having the students go with me. Sometimes I would have two students. I tried to make it interesting and productive for them. I observed them do some of their skills and instructed them on others. One of the places I took them was to the home of two elderly sisters. Known as the "cat women," one of them had a wound that required daily wound care. As we pulled up to the dilapidated old house with boards missing on the front porch, one of the students said, "We're going in there?"

We sat for a minute as I told them about the women. I instructed the students to follow me closely so as to step on the boards that I knew would hold weight. It was so hot in there. The gas space heaters were turned wide open as the little women sat quietly on ragged sofas. The sunlight streamed through the window illuminating the cat hair in the air. We counted nineteen sickly, emaciated cats in their home that morning; one even had its eyeball hanging out of the socket. Cats were everywhere, climbing on the few pieces of furniture they had and on the kitchen counters eating out of the sink. We visiting nurses never took our bag in there, only the necessary supplies. The students really got an education about how some people live. Soon after, a social service organization was able to move the women to a better environment, but they were devastated to leave their cats.

Our agency was prepared for any type of natural disasters. The Blizzard of '93 came through in March, leaving people without power and making for dangerous driving conditions. We had responsibilities to our patients to contact them, making sure they were okay and that their needs were met. Many patients made arrangements leaving their homes to stay with family members. The patients were triaged by acuity, such as requiring oxygen, IVs, or daily dressing changes. If a patient needed transferring to an inpatient facility, we made those arrangements as well.

It was a privilege to provide care to World War II veterans. I easily lost track of time when they told stories of the war, fighting in the Pacific or landing on the beaches of Normandy. My favorite veteran had been in General Patton's army. He had an excellent memory and provided fascinating details of his wartime experiences. He loved to be outside, so he rode about his property on a motorized scooter. Sometimes he would "go missing" so his family would have to get out and look for him. Usually he had gotten his scooter stuck in an old garden rut or mired down in the mud. He was a tough old bird. One word that describes all of my veteran patients: PROUD.

One of my all-time favorite patients lived in a room on the second floor of an old hotel that was well known for its Sunday Buffets, serving the best fried chicken, fresh vegetables and homemade pies in the state of Alabama. My elderly patient had suffered a stroke leaving her unable to speak and walk. It was the weirdest thing, she could feed herself with her "good hand' eating something fried every meal accompanied by a desert. She could swallow fine. She was confined to her bed and a wheelchair, but her skin never broke down. Eating all that high calorie food kept her fluffy, padding her pressure areas.

Many of my home health patients had previously been in the hospital where I worked. I knew most of them and their caregivers. One day I was at the home of a little old man who had emphysema. It was always a great visit. I loved going there. He lived with his daughter and son-in-law. One day the son-in-law reminded me of his life changing hospital admission.

He said, "Do you remember the time I was in the hospital with that bleeding ulcer? You were with Dr. Adams (not his real name) when he told me, 'Boy, you pull this shit again don't call me, call the funeral home!'"

I replied, "Oh yeah, I do remember that!" He went on to say that because the surgeon was so blunt, it saved his life and his marriage because he stopped drinking after that strong and frank warning.

❧

Going out in the field we encountered many different animals, mostly cats and dogs as I have talked about. One patient had a pet bird in a cage that squawked whenever we came in the room. I didn't like that bird and it didn't like me. One of my friends and caregiver to her elderly mother-in-law lived in a huge home on the lake. She loved animals. She raised a baby squirrel in a plastic swimming pool in the bathroom. That was really neat. One of the home health nurses in my office told me she came out of her patient's house to find seven goats standing on her new car. They must have been attracted to the shiny new car. *Can you imagine opening a dresser drawer to gather dressing supplies to find a possum in there?*

Many times I traveled back roads and came upon cows in the road sometimes blocking the route. If no one was out trying to round them up, I'd stop at the nearest house to let someone know.

৵৽৽

Dressing changes was one of the most common skills we provided, and Duoderm was the number one wound care product used in our agency. Surely, I've applied enough Duoderm to patch up the Titanic. Some of the wound tracts I have seen tunneled six inches. All wounds had to heal from the inside, taking months to heal or sometimes never healing. We always double bagged the contaminated dressings and put them in the outside garbage can.

You really never know what is under a dressing, especially in home health. I went to change the dressing of a man that had emergency surgery for a dissecting aortic aneurysm. He had a rather large girth and a big bulky dressing. After some history and an assessment, I gathered my supplies to change the dressing. I removed the dressing layer by layer and got down to the wound packing. I found the end of the packing and began to slowly pull out yards of NuGuaze. *Hummm.* I wondered how deep this wound was. After removing about a mile of packing I got to the bottom. It was deep. I cleaned it, repacked, and dressed it while trying to avoid having any facial expressions.

It seems like the longer I worked in home health care, the more IV therapy I administered, mainly antibiotics. Most often the IV medications and supplies were delivered by an IV home care company. Occasionally, an infusion pump was provided, but usually the medication ran in by gravity. We changed peripheral IV sites every three days unless the patient had some sort of port. It's hard to believe that I gave Dobutamine intravenously in the home. Dobutamine is a drug given to patients with heart failure.

The nurses represented the agency in the community at health fairs, nutrition centers for the elderly, and the Relay for Life. We did blood pressure checks and gave health related programs. One

114

afternoon my supervisor called me to her office asking me to "work a funeral." *What is she talking about?* I wondered.

She explained that one of our African American patient's funeral was that afternoon and she wanted to send two nurses there to tend to any of the family members who might pass out. Another nurse and I were given some smelling salts or ammonia capsules and instructed to keep them in our pockets until they were needed. We arrived at the church and took our place on each side of the front door. After the funeral began we stood just inside the doorway. About midway through the funeral one of the women in the family stood up, raised her hands, yelled something, and passed out. We ran to her, popped one of the ammonia capsules and waved it under her nose, bringing her around. Then other family members did the same thing, one right after the other. I'd never witnessed anything like that. We attended each one and at the end of the funeral they all seemed to be all right.

Until the Balanced Budget Act passed congress in 1997, home health was very lucrative with reimbursements seemingly unlimited. This is the only time in my nursing career I received monetary bonuses. With the new guidelines, visits were decreased and emphasis was placed on the caregivers assuming more of the care such as wound care.

In 1998 before all the new rules and regulations came down, my boss created a position for me at the doctor's office next to the community hospital where I'd worked. It was a great job, kind of cushy. I was excited to work with that group of doctors again. The agency rented a tiny office, which was previously a closet, setting it up with a computer, telephone, and a fax machine. I took calls from the nurses who had patients under the care of the doctors who practiced there. I walked to their office, discussed the patient's issues, typed the orders, updated the med sheet, and made any phone calls to notify the nurse, drug store, or DME supplier. I also had the physicians sign orders and returned them to our office. Soon the huge offices were downsized, the patient census decreased, and offices were consolidated. My wonderful job was over.

I enjoyed my nine years working in home health care. I came to know many good people, saw how they lived, and witnessed the dedication of the caregivers. I gained a new respect for caregivers.

I'd been around them with hospital patients where the nurses and aides were in and out of the room being there to help. In the home, the caregiver—usually a spouse or a child—was there twenty-four hours a day, seven days a week, with only occasional breaks. There was one lady I recall who cared for her homebound mother for years; she rarely left her house. After her mother died she made her first trip to the Winn Dixie. When she walked up to the door to go into the store, the automatic doors slid open and scared her to death. She'd never seen such.

There was a ten-year-old girl that was her bed bound grandmother's caregiver. She and her grandmother shared a room. It was sad for me to see the duties she carried out; cooking and emptying bedpans and potty chairs. Some of the caregivers were paid, and weren't usually family members. They showed unlimited patience and kindness to their patients. Some patients lived alone, managing their own care. I am sure there were some who didn't see another person except the nurse for days. Some of the patients and caregivers were always giving me things, mainly fresh vegetables just picked from their gardens or jars of homemade jellies.

Two things I learned while working with the elderly: you can't change old people and filth won't kill you. I received many rewards working in home care from a hug in the grocery store to the satisfaction of knowing you helped someone stay in their home when they were sick, recovering from surgery, or dying. The best thing that happened to me as a home health nurse was that I met and married my husband. His mother was my patient. The time had come for a change, my girls were older, and I felt like I could go to the city and get a job working in the love of my career obstetrics. Before I applied, I called the California OB for some advice and words of encouragement. After all, it had been seventeen years since I worked as an OB nurse.

He assured me that things were basically the same, only some things had a different name. "You know, Camille, there are only two ways to have a baby."

I applied for a staff nurse position on night shift in Labor and Delivery at a hospital in the city. I was hired February 5th, 2000.

Chapter Eleven

THE PATIENT

I don't like being the patient, even for small stuff like the removal of a mole or sitting in the dentist chair. Nevertheless, the older I get the more I find myself playing the part. Forty seems to be that magic birthday when it all starts to fall apart. Every few years they add some sort of routine test increasing the incidence of finding something. Not only do body parts start wearing out but they grow things that should not be there. If something is found, then they want to do something about it.

One day you're fine and the next you find yourself sitting anxiously in a doctor's office fearing the worst. That day came for me at the age of forty-three when I noticed hematochezia. My home health office at that time shared the building with the gastroenterologist's office, so as soon as I noticed the bleeding, I walked around the corner to his office and told his nurse. It was confirmed and they scheduled me for the dreaded colonoscopy, the first of three. I thought to myself, "I'm too young. This can't be happening to me."

Preparation was the worst part, but I got through it and went to my appointment in the familiar GI lab of the community hospital where I had worked previously. The nurses were friends of mine and gave me plenty of good medicine to make sure I didn't feel a thing. The gastroenterologist found the site of the bleeding and took a biopsy of it. The biopsy was inconclusive so he wanted to repeat the test. *Okay,* I thought.

So the next week I repeated the whole thing again. Afterwards, the doctor told me that I might have to have it removed. Thank Goodness, I was still quite sedated by the Demerol and Versed, otherwise I would have freaked out with that news.

The younger brother of the gastroenterologist happened to be a general surgeon on staff and was consulted to look at the lesion that had been discovered on my colon. Still unsatisfied, the gastroenterologist sent me to yet another doctor for his opinion which meant a third colonoscopy. This doctor was one of the best in the country and luckily he was close by. Years of experience had afforded this physician to see just about everything that could possibly grow inside a colon. After the colonoscopy he said to me, "I don't know what it is, but it has to come out."

NURSE CURSE!

"This must be really bad if he didn't know what it was." I was getting worried. I could envision myself laying there with a long incision on my belly, a nasogastric tube, and a Foley catheter, or even a colostomy. Then there was the possibility of the worse, some rare cancer. Sometimes as a nurse you know too much which really escalates your fears. The expression holds true; ignorance is bliss. The young surgeon told me about a Birmingham surgeon who did colon resections laparoscopically. He'd done some of his training under him and he was one of the best. I had no idea that a laparoscopic colon resection was even an option.

The gastroenterologist made the appointment and sent my records to Birmingham. I went to see this *Godfather* of the laparoscope for an evaluation. It's a very different experience at these big teaching facilities. First, I saw the chief resident. He serves as the assistant to the primary surgeon and, at times, fills the role of the lead physician during surgery. He took my history and did an assessment. When I finally met the "Main Man" I was taken aback. He was old. He had a very no nonsense demeanor. The only good news I got that day was that I didn't have to have a nasogastric tube. Thank, God.

He said, "I'm operating on the other end of your GI tract so, no, you won't need one, but I can give you one if you want it."

My colon resection was scheduled and the nurse handed me printed instructions with several prescriptions.

⊷⊶

As I was leaving she said, "By the way, February 24th is the doctor's birthday."

I sat quietly on the way home, looking over the paperwork, pondering my upcoming surgery. And there was the unknown. *What was that in my colon?* The not-knowing was worrisome and I couldn't stop thinking about it. The week before the surgery, I decided to do something for the surgeon's birthday. I thought about getting somebody to draw a birthday cake on my belly, but I figured he might not even see it. I was sure that I would be asleep and draped when he walked in the operating room. So I decided I'd write him a poem. The words came easy as it flowed together. I had it printed and framed and wrapped it in colorful paper ready to present it to him on the day of my surgery. It was his 65th birthday.

On Friday before my Tuesday operation, I began the necessary preparations. This was my fourth colon prep in a month. No solid foods. Only clear liquids. I also began taking three different antibiotics. I was swallowing a pill every couple of hours. By Sunday, I was getting weak. Then the laxatives were ordered. My husband drove me up on Monday, having to stop frequently at convenience stores along the way. *Is this really happening? Can I do this?* I wanted to run away and forget the whole thing. After checking into the hospital hotel I took the last laxative, a bottle of magnesium citrate. It was like I had the stomach virus all night. It was horrible.

I checked into the hospital at 6 AM. I was ushered into the holding area and guess what they had waiting for me there? A Fleets enema. Finally my bowel was prepped as well as it would ever be, sanitized, sterilized, and empty. I waited on a stretcher holding my gift for the doctor. The nurses and anesthesia people inquired about the package so I told them it was the surgeon's gift for his birthday. They called him to come by the holding area that I wanted to see him. In a few minutes he appeared.

He asked" Did you want to see me?"

I replied "Happy Birthday!" He looked shocked. He stood there for a minute with his hands in his pockets. I gave him his gift. As he opened the present, the OR personnel gathered around. He thanked me for the present and gave me a hug. I read the poem:

Twas the Day of Surgery

Twas the day of surgery, I was at the brink
I'd slept none at all, not even a wink.
The bowel all prepped and sterilized too,
Oh what I'd give for something to chew.

I waited patiently all snug in my bed
While visions of pasta danced in my head.
I tried to relax and take a short nap,
But I was too nervous with my upcoming lap.

When from the OR there arose such a clatter
I sprang from my gurney to see what was the matter.
Away to the door I flew like a flash
I peeked through the window as I grabbed my sash.

The room all polished, neat and bright,
It took my breath to see such a sight!
Instruments all shiny and laid in a row,
Sutures all neatly tied in a bow.

I spied the "good doctor" so lively and quick.
He repairs the body and heals the sick.
Not a big man as I recall,
But on this day he's ten feet tall.

Just as he turned he caught my eye.
It was now my turn and I wanted to cry.
With a squint of his eyes and a twist of his head,
He gave me to know I had nothing to dread.

DUTY SHOES

"Now doctors, now interns and residents too!
On nurses, and techs to name just a few.
Turn up the gas, open the lines,
It's time for this one to go sublime!"

He grasped the scope tight in his hand,
By all accounts he's the best in the land.
With high tech magic he begins his work,
I didn't feel a thing, not even a jerk.

Into the belly with precision and skill,
Around omentum and colon at will.
He cut and stapled, and stapled and cut,
Now it's all over, I have a new gut.

Off with monitors, off with the trodes
Get that number forty out of my nose.
Into recovery with an unconscious smile,
I knew I'd made it, I'd run the last mile.

Wearily, I try to open my eyes.
Who's this face? Is this a disguise?
It's the "good doctor" so meek and so mild
With the strength of a man and the touch of a child.

Wake up, wake up, you're all done.
Take some deep breaths and go have some fun.
I exclaimed when I rolled past the nurse's desk,
"When you've been with Henry, you've been
with the best!"

By: Camille Foshee-Mason
February 24, 1998

After the little party, the anesthesiologist inserted an eighteen gauge cathlon in my hand. Luckily he didn't have to dig around to hit the vein, but it still hurt. He began injecting some Versed into the IV line which took a little of the edge off. The last thing I

121

remember was moving myself over onto the OR table as I looked around the room. I still couldn't believe this was happening to me. The surgery went as planned. I remember nothing about the recovery and that's certainly a good thing.

When I was moved into my room, I was lucid enough to ask, "Where's my PCA pump, I need some of it."

The nurse replied, "He doesn't use them."

What? I couldn't believe it.

The nurse gave me IV Demerol and Phenergan that didn't touch the pain. Dilaudid did the trick. No NG tube, as promised, and no Foley catheter. I got up that night several times to the bathroom. I wore no TED hose.

The doctor and his entourage rounded early the next morning. The first thing he said was, "Mrs. Mason, you've had your appendix removed and you have no adhesions, why is that?"

What? I don't know.

He had a stack of pictures in his hand that he took with the camera of the laparoscope. He gave two of them to me so I could take them to my gastroenterologist. He found an endometrioma, which is a benign cyst that had attached to and eaten through my colon causing it to bleed. I didn't even know that I had endometriosis. He told me that he had seen it a very few times, less than five, as he held up five fingers. He showed some excitement when he discussed it because it was uncommon and he could use it in his teaching.

He removed eight inches of my descending colon. After two days of Dilaudid my tongue began to swell. I walked in the hall many times on Thursday trying to relieve the gas pains in my shoulder and in by belly. By Friday, I was drinking liquids and taking pain medicine by mouth. My first regular diet they served was the noon meal on Saturday before I was discharged. It was fried chicken and turnip greens. Only in the south. Fortunately, I had no complications during my hospital stay.

I had some good nurses while I was there and two that were questionable. Maybe none of them wanted to be assigned to me because I was a nurse. Maybe they drew straws. I don't think I told them, but I'm sure my mother did. I kept thinking that somebody would listen for bowel sounds, but no one ever did. They were always punctual with my pain medication and for that I was grateful. One of the night nurses came in and hung a piggyback of Reglan. After she left the room, my husband noticed something splattering on his shoes. The nurse didn't insert the piggyback into the main line IV and the Reglan just ran on the floor. I didn't say anything. The next night she did the same thing. I finally said something.

I had a conversation with my dayshift nurse as I was complementing my room. It was huge and had an area for sitting in the sun. It was the best patient room I'd ever seen. She told me I was in the VIP suite. How about that? She knew about the poem and said that the surgeon had carried it around with him showing it to the nurses.

Before shift change on Saturday morning this Barbie Doll night nurse came in, complete with long blonde hair, painted nails, and perfect makeup. *Whose makeup is perfect at the end of a shift?* She came in to change my bag of IV fluids. There was half of the bag left, but she disconnected the tubing from the bag to change it out. She couldn't get the tab off the new bag to spike it, probably because of her acrylic nails. She laid the end of the tubing over the top of IV pole and left the room to get someone to remove the tab. I watched the drip chamber run dry and air come down the IV tubing. I pinched the tubing and waited for her to come back. She came back and hung the IV bag.

I said, "Do you see the air in the tubing?" She nodded her head.

"Well are you gonna get it out?"

Obviously, she didn't know what to do. I asked her to go get me an eighteen gauge needle and I would show her how to get the air out. Yep, it was time for me to go home. I hate to sound like "picky nurse turned patient," but hanging piggybacks and changing IV fluids are routine nursing duties.

I had experienced major surgery with the modern laparoscope. I could attest to all of the benefits it boasted rather than with an open abdominal operation.

I did well at home, all systems working. I finally got to examine my two inch incision and the other tiny ones. I saw no stitches so I assumed he glued the skin together. Eight days after my surgery I got the yeast infection from hell. I knew it was coming, I should have been prepared. I sent my husband to Wal-Mart to get one of the many creams. He came back with a tube of athlete's foot medicine. The next day I got a prescription for Diflucan. It's magic. I drove myself to Birmingham to see the surgeon for my follow-up visit. He was so impressed with how well my convalescence was progressing that he took me around his office introducing me as his two week post-op colon resection.

His nurse weighed me that day, I was sure I had lost at least ten pounds. No. I'd only lost two pounds with the whole ordeal. What a disappointment.

Chapter Twelve

MATERNAL CHILD – LABOR and DELIVERY NURSE 2000–PRESENT

I couldn't wait to get started in my new job. The first week of orientation was done at the big-sister hospital across town. This organization ran several medical facilities and all the new hires met in a huge room receiving the same orientation. We had the usual new employee labs drawn, urine test, and TB test. We were divided into groups for computer training. To work in Labor and Delivery it was required that we complete ACLS or Advanced Cardiac Life Support, NRP or Neonatal Resuscitation Program and CPR or Cardiopulmonary Resuscitation. I'd stayed current in CPR since I graduated from nursing school, but had only heard of the dreaded ACLS, this would be my first time taking it. NRP was new to me too. Within weeks I was certified in all three.

Finally, I was done with the preliminaries and began my orientation in the Labor and Delivery Unit. The unit had seven labor and delivery rooms (LDRs) and six small antepartum rooms. Sometimes the antepartum rooms were used as labor and delivery rooms. Patients were triaged in any of these rooms. There were two operating rooms with a three-bed recovery room right in the middle of the unit. The NICU and the well-baby nursery was across the hallway from the OR suites.

I met the doctors and nurses, trying to put faces with names. There were about sixteen obstetricians and three certified nurse midwives (CNM) delivering seventy-five to 100 babies a month at the 150-bed hospital. I knew two of them; one was my GYN and the other one I knew from the eighties when he took call for the California OB.

I was assigned to one of the best Labor and Delivery Nurses for my orientation. I'd never been in an LDR so all of this was new to me. The LDRs were made to be as homelike as possible, with each room being equipped with a sofa, table, chairs, and cabinet for supplies, TV, and rocking chair. On the wall opposite from the labor bed was the infant warmer and next to the bed was the fetal heart monitor. She showed me all through the unit explaining where equipment and supplies were kept. I was given a password to obtain medications from the Pyxis Med Station and one for the use of the computer. We were allowed to wear street clothes in to work then changed into hospital scrubs in the unit locker room. I bought a pair of Anywear duty shoes to match my green scrubs. They didn't leak and could be washed easily. I had a photo ID badge that attached to my scrubs.

On February 15th I got to see my first delivery. After the shift report, we went into the LDR to meet and assess our assigned patient. She was obviously laboring. The patient was connected to the fetal monitor which graphed the fetal heart rate and the contractions. The mother's blood pressure and pulse rate interfaced onto the graph paper. The nurse prepared her for an epidural by increasing the IV fluid to a faster rate, to prevent her blood pressure from dropping. The nurse pulled the anesthetic Naropin and brought the anesthesia cart to the room. After the patient received a liter of fluid, the anesthesiologist came to the bedside, sat the patient up on the side of the bed, and placed the small catheter into her back. He purged the anesthetic through the tubing and connected it to a pump that administered a prescribed amount keeping her comfortable during her entire labor.

We placed a Foley catheter into her bladder to keep her bladder empty. The nurse and I kept a close watch on the fetal monitor strip and her blood pressure. We kept her turned from side to side to facilitate labor and to prevent a drop in her blood pressure. As the patient became comfortable we talked with her and her husband without the pain of contractions. The two of them were so excited to be having their first baby, a girl, named Emily. She progressed to ten centimeters and was ready to push. We called the doctor to report her progress. The nurse turned on the infant warmer, rolled in the covered delivery table, an exam light, and a stool, transforming the labor room into the delivery room. We pulled the stirrups into position from underneath, raised the bed as the bottom half of the bed lowered. We removed the lower half of the bed also known as "breaking the bed." After the Foley was removed, we raised her legs into the stirrups. After a few pushes we could see her little bald head crowning.

The obstetrician arrived as well as the NICU nurses. The NICU nurses attend all premature deliveries and little Emily was arriving six weeks early.

Weighing five pounds seven ounces, she was introduced to the world. She was handed off to the nurses who took her over to the warm bed where they dried her. Soon she was crying and turned pink. They did a newborn assessment, foot printed her, and applied two of the four matching ID bands. The other two went to mama and daddy. What a great feeling to see her birth and return to the world of delivering babies.

She stayed ten days in the NICU to make sure she was '"okay". I went by the NICU and checked on her every day that I worked. The day after she was born, I saw one of the NICU nurses rolling her down the hall in an isolette. I recognized her, and asked the nurse what was going on with her. She told me that she was taking her downstairs to get a CT of her head. Immediately tears welled up in my eyes and I could feel a lump growing in my throat. I had to tell myself that I couldn't be getting upset when a baby had a problem because it would happen. She was fine and progressed nicely in the NICU. Even though she was born a southern belle, she has lived in Portland, Oregon since she was five weeks old. Never fails, I get a Christmas card every year with a picture of Emily and her family.

The unit had centralized monitoring. The antiquated five-by-five inch fetal monitor screens were located at the nurse's station where we could see the strips while at the desk. We charted from the graph paper torn from the bedside monitors. When in the room we typed in or wrote on the strip any pertinent information that was noted or done at the bedside, such as artificial rupture of membranes, SVE, and oxygen. Then, we charted the paper work at the desk.

Every day I continued to learn new things and met new people.

I'd heard of some sort of vacuum that was sometimes used in deliveries, but I'd never seen one. Some of the doctors used a Mityvac to assist in guiding the baby's head out and some used forceps. Occasionally, the doctor or midwife inserted an IUCP or intrauterine pressure catheter into the uterus around the baby's head to monitor the strength of the contractions. I observed and eventually learned to attach an FSE or fetal scalp electrode to the baby's head after the membranes ruptured. This was helpful if there was some question about the fetal heart rate or if the baby was difficult to trace during labor.

I took a few shifts to receive and do the immediate care of the newborn at delivery. I quickly performed the newborn assessment. When I received them, I dried and stimulated them while I counted their toes and fingers. I ran my gloved hand across the roof of their mouth to check for cleft palate. I took a quick look over the body looking for any marks or imperfections. I counted the vessels in their cord. They are normally three: two arteries and one vein. I listened to their heart and lungs counting respirations and the heartbeat. I took an axillary temperature.

As my orientation continued I took on more responsibility and became familiar with the charting. After a few weeks, I took my own labor patient with the nurse available to troubleshoot any problems and learned how to assess triage patients and care for the high risk ones. Then, it was time to get acquainted and function independently in the operating room. I observed a few cases, but I still couldn't watch the initial cut on the skin. I eased into circulating C-sections and post-partum tubal ligations.

One day there happened to be two or three scheduled C-sections and three from the labor floor. I circulated six C-sections one right after the other. That's the best way to learn; by repetition. There were usually two obstetricians that scrubbed making the operation move fast. I couldn't get all my paperwork done by the time they were finished.

The most amazing thing was how well the mothers did in surgery and in recovery. They rarely got sick in the operating room.

Most of them recovered with perfect makeup, the head of the bed elevated, and without a complaint of pain. *How could that be? Good drugs in the OR?*

Most all C-section patients have an epidural or spinal block so they are awake during their surgery, but occasionally one has general anesthesia. The patients no longer have to lie flat after spinal anesthesia as they did back in the '70s and '80s because a small spinal needle is used causing less leakage of spinal fluid. Unless they were allergic to Morphine, they were given Duramorph with their blocks.

By the end of my twelve week orientation, I felt I could function as a L&D nurse. The California OB was right. Few things had changed, but, yes, different terms were used.

I'd not heard of Group B Strept (GBS) testing or the prophylaxis used to prevent it. Most of the obstetricians and midwives do a vaginal swab for GBS on the mother at her thirty-sixth week prenatal visit. We get the results of this test from the patient's prenatal record. Mothers testing positive are treated with the antibiotics Ampicillin or Clindamycin during labor to prevent the newborn from getting this life-threating infection. If the patient was not tested, they are treated for it anyway.

Back in the day there was no Cytotec or Hemabate for post-partum hemorrhage. We gave Methergine and Pitocin. I recall rubbing boggy uteri off and on for hours keeping it firm preventing hemorrhage. After delivery, if the uterus was boggy the patient bled more clots can form. Back in the day we massaged those boggy uteri to keep them firm.

The first time I saw the IM injection, Hemabate, given it caused massive diarrhea, chills and fever. It was as if the patient had a stomach virus. If the patient is still under the influence of her epidural, it can be a real mess. The OBs order Cytotec more often than Hemabate these days. It's cheap and it works well. I've always been told that redheads have a higher incidence of bleeding, so I've always been mindful of that after one delivers.

I began my eighteen months of the night shift in May working 7 PM to 7 AM. I wanted to return to obstetrical nursing enough that I was willing to go back to the night shift. In preparation, I bought blackout curtains to darken the room and removed the phone from our bedroom. I really liked the work of the nightshift. It wasn't as

129

busy as the day shift and there were less doctors to deal with, but it was hard to sleep in the day. I've never slept well since that year and a half of nights. I liked the nurses and techs I worked with. We usually had a charge nurse and two nurses with one tech. The techs assisted in the deliveries, scrubbed the sections, worked as the unit clerk, and stocked supplies in the LDRs and ORs. They were wonderful and they were very helpful to me. They ordered labs on the computer so I never really had to use it. The Physicians orders were faxed to the pharmacy. Usually, at night, one of the CRNAs, or nurse anesthetist, worked with us placing and managing the epidurals. All of them were good at what they did, reassuring, and kind to the patients. One thing I remember about them, they never complained, even when awaked in the night. Back then we kind of chose our patients, I usually asked for the midwife patients. They were very similar in the way they managed laboring patients and easy to work with. They were very patient with me and taught me "tricks of the trade".

Even with my prior OB experience, I'd never encountered some of the firsts that happened during my time on nights. My first shoulder dystocia happened soon after I started the night shift. I went in to receive the baby of a midwife's patient. She delivered the head and the rest didn't come. We called for help and immediately nurses came to the bedside as we laid the head of the bed flat and opened her pelvis by hyper-flexing her legs. This is called the McRoberts maneuver. The nurses got in position and gave supra pubic pressure as the midwife manipulated the baby and finally delivered the big girl. She was a little stunned, but came around with drying, stimulation, and a little oxygen. The midwife was red faced and sweating. I will never forget what she said when she came out of that room, "Damn, I'm getting too old for this."

One night the unit had been particularly busy, the obstetrician had gone to the call room around 3 AM. I was laboring a patient that was about three centimeters dilated upon admission. I checked her progress with a SVE around 3:30 AM and was surprised to feel something other than a head. I felt around in there trying to figure out what the presenting part was, as she was now dilated about eight centimeters. It was a knee, I was sure of it, but I had to call the doctor who had probably just gone to sleep. I woke him up and gave the report saying, "I think it's a knee"

He replied, "You think it's a knee?"

"Yes, sir."

"Well, it better be," and he hung up the phone. He soon came in and checked her, looked at me and said, "Get her ready for a section!" It was a knee.

I don't know if the hospital had the prison contract or an OB practice had the contract, but we labored and delivered inmates from a women's prison while I was on nights. I'd never been around prisoners before. Their guard was always right outside the door. Some were shackled to the bed, but were released when in good labor. They were always alone and of course they couldn't take their babies with them when discharged. Sometimes we might hear why they were in prison, but most of the time we didn't know.

Since I'm bragging on this, it'll probably happen to me the next time I work L&D. This is the story of my one and only cord prolapse on one of my assigned labor patients. I did an early morning admission of a patient for an induction of labor. Consents signed, blood drawn with IV, assessment, paper work done. The obstetrician talked to the patient as I handed him an amnihook to rupture her membranes.

As he broke her water, he looked at me and said, "Well I have about four inches of cord in my hand."

What? I immediately hit the leaver on the bed and tilted her in the Trendelenburg position as I called for help. That baby's heart rate never faltered, nobody rode the bed. We rolled her to the back for an emergency section.

"Good baby, good mama."

A cerclage is placed for cervical incompetence in early pregnancy, usually after a couple of miscarriages. I'd never heard of a "rescue cerclage," but learned quickly how to assist in doing one. The primip was admitted to the labor and delivery with a dilated cervix with funneling membranes. Her gestational age was less than twenty weeks. We kept her in Trendelenburg position to allow gravity to reduce the membranes. She was taken to the OR in the middle of the night in an attempt to close her cervix. It's a very risky procedure because the membranes are so prominent. As the OB attempted to close the cervix, the membranes ruptured.

My worst experience on the night shift involved a uterine rupture. I was sitting at the nurse's station charting and happened to

131

look up and saw two men standing next to a woman on a stretcher. They were not wearing paramedic uniforms so I didn't know who they were. They told me where they were from and that the woman was twenty-seven weeks pregnant complaining of constipation and abdominal pain. I asked the resident who was hanging out at the desk if he wanted to come along. I led them down the hall to one of the LDRs. I could tell there was something seriously wrong here. She was sweating profusely. I'd only seen that with a "heart attack." She had on so many long heavy clothes I had to cut them off of her to assess her. She was writhing in pain without any vaginal bleeding. The resident connected her to the fetal monitor as I was trying to get labs and get an IV line in her. She was wet with sweat; tape wouldn't stick to her skin so I had to hold the IV in place as I began bolusing fluids in her. The resident called the OB on call from the bedside giving her a detailed report as she was on her way from another hospital. We called for the ultrasound machine to be brought to the bedside and alerted the CRNA who was putting in an epidural for a labor patient across the hall. The OB got there quickly, scanned her and took her directly to the OR for a section. The anesthesiologist inserted a big bore needle into her jugular vein for IV fluids and blood. I held it in place until she was stabilized and stopped sweating. For some reason her uterus ruptured causing this life threatening hemorrhaging. The OB worked fast to control her bleeding, performing a hysterectomy. Soon after the case was started, one of the OBs came from home to assist wearing his house shoes. I saw that night how quickly things can happen on this unit. Like in the ER, you always have to be ready for any emergency. I also saw how swiftly the doctors reacted to this emergency and saved the patient's life. Unfortunately, the baby had died in utero. The two men were apparently ambulance attendants, but were not dressed in uniform. They wore lab coats over their street clothes.

My best night shift experience was the night I labored three patients and delivered three patients. I was so proud. I loved my job.

Some nights were slower than others, sometimes very slow. It was hard to stay awake so we would get up and walk or find something to do. We liked to eat at all hours. They kept it cold in our department, especially the operating rooms. When I had a few minutes to sit down I would go get one of the blankets out of the warmer and wrap up in it. If felt so good but it made me sleepy. Sometimes we got a baby from the adjacent nursery and brought it to the nurse's station where we fed and cuddled it. The unit would get busy around 5 AM with Pitocin induction admissions.

Finally, I came to days, 7 AM to 7 PM, with a new rotation of nurses and techs. One of the nurses was male. I thought that was a little weird, but he did a great job. I got in sync with the day shift. I loved my job so much and told everybody that asked how wonderful it was. Our unit increased its number of patients every year and it seemed like a new OB came on board with one of the groups every year. They were so young. One of the obstetricians who came seemed familiar to me. *Where had I heard his name before?* I soon found out that he was from my neck of the woods and remembered him working in the operating room at my previous hospital in the late eighties. He was a member of my former hospital family.

Between 6 AM and 9AM most of the OBs and midwives made rounds, broke water, and did their scheduled C-sections.

I never knew how my day would go, anything could happen. I tried to keep up with my charting, not getting behind where I wouldn't have to stay after my shift. The nurses and techs were flexible and responded instantly to any situation such as an emergency or an influx of patients. Whether it's true or not, a full moon or a front coming through has always been said to cause patients to go in labor. Sometimes I think it does.

It didn't take many shifts working there before I realized that there were a lot of women with toxemia of pregnancy nowadays. I saw it happening at different gestational ages. I was assigned to a preterm primip who was getting sick with preeclampsia. She was thirty weeks and five days gestation. She needed to be delivered so I was giving her Pitocin to induce labor and Magnesium Sulfate to prevent seizures from her high blood pressure. Sometimes the Magnesium works against the Pitocin making it difficult to start and progress labor. Her hourly tea- colored urine output was dwindling. She had hyper reflexes and a bad headache. I was giving her IV Apresoline and Labetalol to keep her blood pressure below the critical range.

She was getting worse by the hour, so the young OB came in,

assessed her, and decided to deliver her by Caesarean section. I've never seen a doctor do what he did next. He motioned for me and the family to come together in a circle. All of us held hands as he prayed for the young mother, the baby, the family and for the doctors and nurses that would be attending to them. What a comfort to the family and me. I circulated the C-section, recovered her, and watched her closely the rest of my shift as she continued to get the Magnesium and remained very sick. Baby Tapley weighed two pounds ten ounces with a length of fifteen inches. He spent seven weeks in the NICU. From this experience his young mother was instrumental in forming the "Footprints Ministry" at our NICU and currently there are three chapters in the state. These are baby Tapley's footprints taken when he was born, so tiny, and so perfect.

TAPLEY"S FOOTPRINTS
(not actual size)

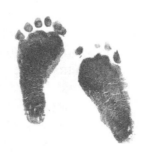

He's eleven years old now and recently completed fourteen productions of "To Kill a Mockingbird" as the character Dill at the Alabama Shakespeare Festival.

It so happened that both of my daughters were expecting babies in the spring of 2003 and of course they were to deliver at my hospital. As the time got closer, I began to think of all the things that could happen, making me a little nervous. As do most couples, they knew the baby's sex and they both had names way before they were born. My youngest daughter was due first and was expecting a girl, Alexis, and my oldest daughter was expecting a boy, Baxlee, five weeks later.

For nine months, all I did was work with, talk about, and watch pregnant women on TV. When I went to their homes they were always watching *The Baby Channel*. One day my youngest daughter called me at work saying, "I haven't felt Lexi move today."

Immediately, a sick feeling came over me. I tried to be reassuring to her on the phone and told her to come in and we'd check her out. I went straight to my manager, about to cry, and asked her if she would assess her when she arrived. Everything was fine with her, I guess baby Lexi was sleeping in that morning.

My oldest daughter had to go on bed rest early on due to contractions, probably because she didn't drink enough water while teaching school all day.

Lexi was born at forty weeks and Baxlee at thirty-eight weeks both with Pitocin induction and epidural anesthesia. What a blessing. Both had uneventful childbirth experiences and perfect babies.

From the beginning of time, women have had their babies naturally. It's an option. There are three situations of natural childbirth that I've seen. In the first circumstance, the woman prefers natural childbirth. She has prepared herself and uses relaxation and breathing techniques to reach her goals. Sometimes the patient brings a doula or labor coach with her who assists her in laboring. They provide encouragement, support, and reassurance and comfort measures during labor. Some of the patients labor on a birthing ball. When you see someone stepping off the elevator with one of those you know they are "a natural patient." The prepared natural patients are more likely to bring in a birth plan. Some requests I've seen on a birth plan include walking during labor, no pain medicines, cutting the umbilical cord after the cord stops pulsating, holding and nursing the baby immediately after birth. Our unit does try and accommodate birth plans. I've had couples ask to take their placenta home with them.

In the second scenario, the patient is afraid of needles. Some of them will take IV pain medicine, Stadol, Nubain, or Phenergan but no epidural because of a *needle* being put in their back. Most of them have heard a horror story about an epidural and won't change their minds. They're the screamers.

Thirdly, there are those fast laboring patients that come in almost completely dilated begging for an epidural. I hate it when that happens. The patient is so disappointed because it's too late for an epidural. Often they deliver their babies soon after arriving when this happens; the labor nurse goes into the "you can do it" mode. We get them focused, we reassure them, and we coach them through it.

One morning I received my written assignment to labor a midwife's patient, a primip. The names of the patients were written on a huge board, behind the nurse's station, out of the site of visitors of course. My patient's last name was one I'd never forgotten from a previous delivery many years ago. In the comment square was written, her mother died with HELLP syndrome. *Could this girl be the baby of the patient with DIC that we sent to Birmingham twenty something years ago?*

I walked in her room noticing three women about my age with her. I introduced myself and the patient told me some things about herself. I asked her if she was born at the community hospital and if her mother was sent to Birmingham and died.

Those women stood up and asked "How did you know that?"

I explained that I was there that morning, readied her mama for surgery, went with her to the OR, and received her, pointing to the patient, when she was born. They couldn't believe it and I couldn't either. Sometimes things come full circle. The ladies were so appreciative of everything that was done for her and had so many good things to say about the California OB. The young woman, Jessica   did great with her labor and delivery. What an honor to be her nurse.

The patient load continued to increase and every few years there was an expansion adding more LDRs and remodeling some of the existing rooms. With more patients came more doctors, more nurses, more techs and my second computer challenge.

In October of 2003, the new computer system, we call QS, was introduced. It was exclusive to labor and delivery including triage and antepartum. There was so much to learn. I attended computer classes and received help from the "super users." I was a fifty-year-old computer alien, unlike many of the young nurses I worked with. They were such fast learners zipping from screen to screen thinking that all of us "seasoned" nurses could pick it up after showing us a couple of times. Wrong. Frustration and repetition is how I learned it.

After a few weeks I knew what a good thing this computer system was. It bridged with our fetal heart monitors and interfaced everything that was typed in at a computer at the bedside or at a nurse's desk. There were large detailed screens at the nurse's station that displayed the fetal monitor strips for each room. The patient's vital signs rolled across the screen also. The system also had a chalkboard screen that was updated regularly showing patient names, G/P, doctor, SVE and diagnosis making it easier for the doctors and the charge nurse to keep up with each patient. This did away with the hand written dry erase board. The delivery record, progress notes, and admission paperwork were generated from the QS was printed and kept in a hard chart. Even now when the system has to be upgraded causing it to be down, it's a hassle to gather and complete the paperwork that we previously did.

The biggest baby I recall being born at this hospital weighed twelve pounds three ounces and I labored the mama. It never occurred to me that she might not be able to deliver him; she was six feet tall. She had such a long torso that her belly didn't look that big and usually the taller ones have the least trouble delivering.

When I came to work the next day I learned that she was sectioned after I left. I went to the nursery to see this "big boy." He was huge, taking up the whole newborn bed. That night I saw a preview of the local news that was going to do a story on the big baby so I rounded up some of the nurses, techs, and the moms attending OB and we watched the video in an empty room. That baby was alert. He sat in his daddy's lap looking like a three-month-old as his parents were interviewed. We all chuckled as we watched.

When learning to do SVEs or sterile vaginal exams. I learned presentation, dilation, effacement, and station. Sometimes, if the presenting part is not in the pelvis, it's hard to assess. I have a hard time even reaching the cervix—my fingers are short. When assessing the cervix, I have had a little hand grab my fingers or felt some tiny toes wiggle when I touch them. If I think it's a head, I am mindful of suture lines making sure it is indeed a head. Every now and then on the unit, one would slip by and the patient would be almost completely dilated before discovering the baby was breech. In that case, the patient is whisked to the OR for a C-section.

In 2006, I had labored a G3 P2 all morning. Shortly after lunch she had completely dilated, so I asked her to give me a push to see if the head moved down, giving me an idea of how the pushing was going to go. I was sure that I felt the suture line. She brought the head down with that push so I called the OB to come for delivery. She was blocked, comfortable, and there was no hurry, the baby looked fine on the monitor. I had everybody and everything in place for a routine vaginal delivery when the OB came in. He gowned, gloved and took his place as I held one leg and the daddy held the other. She gave a big push and the baby's boy parts plopped out.

I gasped as the daddy asked, "What's that?"

The OB replied, "Testicles."

"Oh, shit," I said to myself.

The OB did a beautiful breech delivery, it looked effortless. As the OB left the room he gave me one of his smirky smiles. I guess that suture line I was feeling was the baby's butt crack. You gotta watch out for those *butt cracks*; they can fool you.

Grandbaby number three was due in October 2006. The OB scheduled the induction at forty weeks. My daughter was admitted around three in the afternoon for Cytotec since she is one of those that has a cervix of steel and just doesn't go into labor without it. She had a dose and was contracting by the time I left, but they didn't seem to bother her as she was eating a big supper. Around ten that evening I was awakened by the charge nurse calling to tell me that she was five centimeters dilated and bolusing for an epidural. She got a little dose of labor before getting her epidural. By midnight she was completely dilated, but the head was still high, so the nurses let her "labor down" for a couple of hours. At 2 AM our little Lily was born.

The OB began the delivery. "Oh, she has a veil. They say that they have the sixth sense," she announced as she pulled the amniotic membrane off of her head.

Babies born in a veil, or caul, is a rare occurrence. Maybe one in a thousand. In medieval legends it was a sign of good luck for a child to be born in a caul. She was beautiful.

By 2007, our unit needed another expansion. In 2008, we proudly opened our new unit boasting fifteen LDRS, one antepartum bed and a new four-bed post anesthesia care unit (PACU). A brand new spacious OR was also added giving us three operating rooms. We had grown into a huge unit and it was clear we were running with the big dogs now.

The six bed triage unit and six bed antepartum, or high risk obstetrical unit, had opened the year before allowing more beds for labor patients. Again, there were more doctors, more nurses and more staff to attend to the increase in patients. There were some of the nurses that primarily stayed in triage, antepartum, or the OR, but others of us rotated thorough all of them.

Working in a city hospital exposed me to many foreign cultures, ones I wasn't accustomed to. There are many Hispanic patients that delivered at our hospital. I didn't speak or understand Spanish, but I've learned two words in the past thirteen years, *dolor*, meaning "pain," and *empujar*, meaning "push." One of the OBs and one of the midwives spoke Spanish fluently. We've had a few nurses over the years that could communicate with Spanish speaking patients.

I remember one Hispanic patient in particular that I labored. She was a twenty-year-old girl from Guatemala having her first baby. She rode a bus from California to Alabama speaking very little English. She was alone and frightened. *How in the world did she get to Alabama and why?* Luckily, her baby was term and did well.

One weekend the ER nurse flew up to our unit pushing a Hispanic woman who was in a wheelchair doubled over in pain. We thought she was about to deliver. We helped her onto the labor bed and began searching for heart tones. We asked the patient and her husband questions using the word baby.

He answered with a confused look on his face, "Baby! No baby!"

She had appendicitis and was promptly taken downstairs to the main OR.

A few years ago our hospital installed a language line on all units to bridge language communication barriers. Some cultural practices only allow female obstetricians, so they choose female obstetricians or midwives to deliver them. Some of the mothers ate special foods and drank special tea after delivery. I can't imagine having a baby in another country where communication is a problem. I think about that when I attend to them.

I'd never worked with residents in my previous jobs. Each year a new batch of them arrived, most of them were my daughters' ages, doing rotations in and out of our unit for three years. They came from all over the world. I had a hard time understanding them sometimes, due to their accents. I found it interesting when they spoke of where they were from and how they got here. One came from Cuba on a raft. We had some "home grown residents" who were undeniably southern complete with Skoal can in pocket.

The residency program was affiliated with our hospital and one of the large OB groups. They had their own patients managing their care in clinic and the hospital. They had a certain quota of deliveries they had to do to complete their program.

❦❧

In 2007, Brooks, grandbaby number four was born. I was on my way home after a twelve hour L&D shift when I got the call, that my oldest daughter's water broke at thirty-eight weeks and they were on their way to L&D. I turned around and headed back to the hospital. She labored all night and right at shift change, the baby's heart tones decelerated for several minutes, which almost bought her an emergency C-section. The nurses and OB burst into her room to assess the situation. I couldn't believe this was happening. I held my breath as that little heart beat slowly, but surely, came back up to normal.

She was completely dilated and the OB took a Kiwi vacuum and guided him out. He was crying, red-faced, and red-headed. I thought it was Betadine on his head. We really don't see many red-headed newborns. One of the OBs must have seen my concern with the monitor strip. He tore the strip from the monitor and called me aside, reviewing it with me.

He said, "You see all this variability this baby has? He's fine."

He'll never know how much those encouraging words meant to me. He was right. My precious Brooks is *tops* in his kindergarten class.

On occasion, I'd come into work and have a couple ask for me to labor them. Sometimes I didn't know them, but most of the time it was someone that I knew from my hometown. There were some

140

of the nurses that were reluctant to do that. It really never bothered me. I've labored many of my daughter's friends and attended their deliveries. There have been many mornings on my day off that I came in to receive the baby in a C-section at a friend or patient's request. Most of the time, the labors, deliveries or C-sections went perfectly, but there have been a few that caused concern, leading into an emergency situation.

One particular patient comes to mind. A laboring primagravida grew up across the street from me and babysat my children, so I knew her well. She was comfortable from her epidural and her labor was progressing as planned. We kept our patients tilted with pillows, keeping them off of their backs helping to stabilize the patient's blood pressure. While inserting the Foley catheter, the heart tones decelerated. I began turning her to try and correct the heart tones. All at the same time, I called for help, turned off the Pitocin, put on oxygen, and opened the IV fluids to a bolus rate. Nothing helped. The patient's mother, one of my best friends, remained calm, but we were certainly "reading one another." Soon the nurses came in and disconnected her from the monitors. We ran down the hall pushing the labor bed. We met the OB in the OR. My heart was pounding as we pulled her onto the OR table. In no time the lifeless baby was handed to the NICU nurse. His first Apgar score was one, meaning there was a heartbeat less than 100. The nurses worked on him as I prayed for him to breathe. They quickly resuscitated him and he was crying in no time. I carried him down the OR hallway to his family waiting in the hall. With tears in my eyes I handed him to his daddy. Gabe is a straight A student in the sixth grade.

As an L&D nurse, sooner or later, you *will* deliver a baby. I always try to get the doctor there in time, but sometimes there are those babies that just slide on out. We call them a precipitous delivery, or precip. When the OB burst into the room and the baby is crying I just look at them and reply, "Sorry."

After some experience you know which patients have a higher incidence of a precipitous delivery by obtaining the patients history, G/P, length of previous labors, and weights of previous babies. Then a cervical exam is done and you can tell if there is a lot of room or if it's a tight fit. Ask if they are planning a natural delivery or if they plan to get an epidural. Natural patients tend to precip more often that the "blocked "patients". If I think one is going to precip, I don't" break the bed" just in case. Babies are mighty wet and slippery. I have barehanded precip deliveries years ago, but now I *always* put on gloves. Once the head delivers we check for a cord and if there is one, we try and pull it over the baby's head.

さ・ら

As you may know, Alabama is right in the heart of SEC football. During football season the nurses wear their school colors and catch glimpses of the games when coming in and out of patient rooms. Most babies are "declared" when they are born, usually for The University of Alabama or Auburn University. They wear AU or UA stocking caps not only to keep their heads warm, but to show the teams they will be raised to root for. Some of the dads are decked out with college tee shirts and caps, others are more subtle with a just an emblem on their shirts or belts. On big game days sometimes the nurses bring in food and we set up our own tailgate lunch.

さ・ら

What a comfort to have our Neonatal Intensive Care Unit next door to the L&D unit. We have an amazing group of doctors and nurses. Sometimes when I worked the night shift and L&D was slow, I would go and see the tiny babies. There little legs were the size of my finger. Some of them were connected to tubes and machines. I could never work in there. It would be too stressful caring for those sick and tiny babies

さ・ら

After spending time in the NICU, some of the babies are moved to the Extended Care Nursery also known as the "Feeders and Growers" where they learn to eat and gain weight. Over the past thirteen years the NICU has grown and now there are Neonatal Nurse Practitioners that work with the Neonatologists and the nurses. Because of the close proximity of the NICU to L&D, the nurses quickly respond to newborn emergencies. They attend any delivery that the L&D nurse has called them to, such as prematurity, meconium stained amniotic fluid, and fetal distress. They also respond to all unexpected newborn emergencies. The L&D staff has the NICU number etched in our brains

What could be better that seeing the birth of a baby? The birth of two babies or even three babies. With the use of fertility drugs, such as Clomid, and other infertility measures we have many twins born in our unit.

The OBs take into consideration the position of the babies as to whether they labor or just have a C-section. If the babies are both head down (vertex, vertex) they can delivery vaginally. If the first one is head down and the second is breech many times the patient has a C-section. If the twins are breech they are born by C-section.

All laboring mothers with twins are transported to the OR when pushing begins, in case the need of a C-section arises. There are two OBs in the OR for these deliveries, after the first baby is born; an OB scans the position of the second with an ultrasound. The first born is labeled Baby A, the second, Baby B, and the third one Baby C. I have only seen one set of triplets born. It was amazing. With today's ultrasounds the OBS can determine if they're in two separate sacks or bags of water, one sack, or one placenta. During prenatal visits doctors closely assess and monitor these high risk pregnancies.

My last twin delivery was two years ago, at thirty-two weeks gestation. The young G1 P0 called me at home on a Sunday night saying, 'Miss Camille, I think my water just broke!"

I asked her a few questions and told her she needed to call the OB on call for her group and prepare to go to the hospital to have her complaint checked out. Sure enough her water was broken and she was admitted to L&D with steroids and antibiotics. She was assigned to me the next day and she did go into labor. We took her back for a C-section delivering fraternal twin girls weighing four pounds eleven ounces and five pounds and nine ounces. These were big twins for thirty-two weeks. The NICU nurses commented on their exceptional weights. Carolina and Carleigh stayed ten days in the NICU.

I've only attended one twin delivery with natural childbirth. Now, that was a *real woman*.

Multiple gestation carries a higher risk of preterm labor and many are put on bed rest at home early on in their pregnancies. A

143

rare complication of identical twins is Twin-to-Twin Transfusion Syndrome or TTTS where the two babies share circulation from the single placenta resulting in a "donor twin" that becomes anemic with decreased amniotic fluid and a "recipient twin." that has circulatory overload and increased amniotic fluid. Severe TTTS has a high mortality rate. I'd never heard of this until...

❧

All of their friends were excited to hear the news that the young couple was having twins. This was the second pregnancy for the mother having had a C-section with her first baby. Everything was going well with the exception of morning sickness until the twenty week ultrasound raised some concern because one of the babies had so much more amniotic fluid than the other. She was sent to a perinatoligists who confirmed a diagnosis of Twin-to-Twin Transfusion Syndrome. He named the donor twin "Stuck" and the recipient twin "Poly." He did an amnioreduction from the fluid sack that held "Poly." At twenty-one weeks the couple traveled to Cincinnati where doctors did laser surgery to correct the circulatory defect in the placenta. While the doctors there deemed the procedure a success they told them the outcome was unpredictable and gave them no guarantee. The mother remained home on bed rest only leaving home for doctor's appointments. Each week following her doctor's appointments we were updated on their progress and everyone seemed to be encouraged.

At a thirty-two week ultrasound during a perinatologist visit they were told the worst, little Stuck had died. After 2 days of test and monitoring, they came home to deal with the loss of one baby and an increased worry for the other one. At her regular OB appointment the OB decided to do a C-section. I was off that day, but came in to help with her section, support her and her family. That morning her husband had his gallbladder removed so he was unable to be with her. Her nurse mother, a friend of mine, went into the OR with her. Luke and Landon were born a minute apart. It was truly a time of happiness and sadness with both emotions intertwined in our hearts. I took Landon from the OB lying him on the bed while the NICU nurses worked on his brother. I cleaned him a bit, foot printed him, and wrapped him in blanket with a little stocking cap. After her recovery time, we maneuvered the stretcher through the NICU and let her touch little Luke.

Heartbreakingly, we have our share of stillbirths. Today, they call them intrauterine fetal demise or IUFD. They seem to come in threes. Sometimes a problem is found on an ultrasound making the baby a high risk for demise, others may have no fetal heart beat at a routine office visit. It's awful to go through labor or a C-section and have no baby to take home.

With these patients I stay focused on my work, show sympathy and compassion, but at the same time separate myself from the situation. If I ever cross the line, and lose it, I find myself unable to function and might as well go home. That has happened to me twice in my career, both with stillbirths. After a demise delivery, the mother and father may hold the baby as long as they want. We bathe, dress and take pictures of the baby. The parents are given a memory box of pictures, footprints, a lock of hair and literature. Case management and the hospital chaplain are notified. We transfer them to another unit of the hospital instead of post-partum.

Sometimes babies are so wound up in their umbilical cords that I think "how lucky is this baby." I have seen the umbilical cord wrapped tightly around their necks two and three times. This is referred to as a nuchal cord. Sometimes it can be slipped over the baby's head and sometimes it's so tight it has to be cut before the rest of the baby can be delivered. One day, we noticed a true knot in the cord at delivery.

I was at my computer, when I heard the OB say, "Hey, Camille," and motioned for me.

A few inches from the placenta was a second true knot. I've seen the cord break, causing the OB to quickly clamp both ends of the cord splattering blood everywhere. I've witnessed multiple knots in the umbilical cords of monoamniotic twins delivered by C-section. Monoamniotic means the twins were in the same amniotic sack enabling them to flip and flop entangling their umbilical cords. Yes, sometimes it's a miracle some of them make it.

❧

My fifth grandchild was born at forty weeks gestation in 2010. It was fast, painless, and perfect. My daughter and her husband arrived at the hospital at 6:30 AM. Her IV was started and after assessing a thirty minute fetal monitor strip she was given a dose of Cytotec. The CRNA placed her epidural, the OB broke her water, and by noon she was nursing her big boy Hampton. After her epidural wore off she was ready to go home. Childbirth comes so easy to her.

꼬ᆇ

I have labored my share of VBAC s the past thirteen years. VBAC stands for Vaginal Birth after Cesarean. I have labored some perfect ones and ones that have ended in an emergency Cesarean Section. We now require the mother who intends to VBAC to sign consent. The problem with a VBAC is that the mother has a scarred uterus from a previous C-section and there is no way that anyone can know how it will hold up during labor. Many times I've heard the OB say in the midst of a repeat C-section, "It's a good thing we went ahead with the section because your scar is opening" or "you have a very thin lower uterine segment." Sometimes the laboring mother has pain from the scarring and some of them show signs of fetal distress. Seems like when things go bad with a VBAC they go bad fast and it becomes a stat C-section. Personally, I have been involved in enough VBACs ending up in the OR, that I would discourage anyone from doing it.

Many days are busy and prove quite intense. There are mornings we arrive for work or leave at the end of our shift with every room full. Some days there are several scheduled C-sections and others are brought to the OR from L&D, triage, or antepartum. You never know how it's going to go. L&D nurses and techs are flexible and ready for an emergency that might arise such as emergency C-sections, usually from fetal distress in labor or a severe pre-eclamptic mother.

I can't say enough about our L&D nurses. Most of them are young, energetic, and eager, showing much pride in their work. They really go "the extra mile" in the care of their patients. Not only are they at the bedside with hands-on duties, but they also have to chart it all either at the bedside or the nurse's desk. When a patient is given Pitocin, we chart fetal heart tones every fifteen minutes. Fetal heart tones are charted every five minutes when the patient is pushing and sometimes they might push a couple of hours.

The charge nurses are awesome. I can only hope that at one time I was as good as they are. Some of the L&D nurses have RNC after their name. It stands for Registered Nurse Certified. They've passed the national certification for their specialty of obstetrics.

Interestingly, many of the medications that are used on pregnant women are primarily used for other medical reasons. For instance, we give Brethine, or Terbutaline, to stop contractions in preterm labor. For years I saw it used for bronchospasms in the treatment of asthma. Indocin is an anti-inflammatory drug used in the treatment of rheumatoid arthritis and we give it for preterm labor. Cytotec is utilized for the prevention of gastric ulcers. We use it to soften the cervix prior to labor inductions and for post-partum hemorrhage. Procardia, an antihypertensive is used as a tocolytic in the treatment of preterm labor.

There have been many times when I worked Med-Surg that I've poked a hole in a Procardia capsule squirting the medicine under the tongue of a patient with acutely high blood pressure. Epsom salts is used for many medicinal purposes such as a laxative or in the treatment of sprains, or muscle injuries. Given intravenously as Magnesium Sulfate it is used to relax smooth muscle in preterm labor and to prevent seizures in the pre-eclamptic patient.

Until I went PRN in 2007, I oriented new nurses to the unit. I really enjoyed meeting new nurses and teaching our ways of doing things. If there was a nurse with L&D experience all I had to show them was "the lay of the land" and instruct them on how the OBs liked doing things. Most of the new graduates took somewhat longer, but most seemed to grasp things fairly easily. Occasionally, there would be one that came through that decided L&D wasn't for her.

My take on orientation is that the same nurse needs to do the entire orientation instead of one here and one there, that way nothing is missed. One thing that I've noticed about the new graduates is that they're often hesitant to give IM medications. Nowadays, we give more medications IV than IM so they don't feel as uncomfortable.

One day when IM Celestone was ordered a new grad said to me, "See one, do one."

She observed me do the first injection and she gave the second one the next day. Some of our techs go to nursing school while working in our unit. Many of them return as L&D nurses when finished. They have an added skill set that most nurses don't have. They can scrub C-sections.

❧

We advocate family involvement and our unit is a family-centered unit. A laboring mother can have up to five visitors in her room at her discretion and three in attendance when she delivers. Many times the FOB (father of the baby) helps the nurse turn or reposition the mother during labor. Some of the FOBs are very in tune with the mothers. Some are young and really don't know what to do or what to expect.

If the baby is all right at delivery they are placed on the mother's abdomen and the FOB cuts the cord. The mother holds the baby for the first time. Shortly, the nurse takes the baby to the warmer for assessment, identification, and footprints, and then brought back to the mother for skin-to-skin contact. We encourage all of our mothers in this practice. We also encourage breast feeding and lactation nurses are available. From what I've observed, those mothers who are confident and knowledgeable of breastfeeding do well and the babies latch on easily. In situations where the mother hasn't decided at the time of deliver, saying, "I think I'm gonna try breast feeding," neither the mama nor the baby will do as well with it.

Cameras are allowed in L&D and the OR. After a while the family members, especially siblings come into the LDR to see and hold the newborn for the first time. I will never forget one sibling who came in to see his little sister. He was maybe eight years old. He wore khaki dress pants, a navy blazer, and a tie. His dark hair was combed perfectly. He was such a proud big brother, so well-mannered and soft spoken.

❧

The FOB is allowed into the OR for cesarean sections unless, for some reason, the mother has to receive general anesthesia. After the baby is assessed, foot printed, and ID'd, it's wrapped in warm blankets and held to the mothers face. The FOB, SO (significant other), or family member accompanies the baby's nurse to the nursery while the operation is completed. If the newborn checks out normally, it is brought to the PACU for skin-to-skin contact with the mother for breast feeding, with the FOB at the bedside.

After a recovery period of at least an hour from a vaginal delivery or C-section, the mother is transported to the post-partum floor. Previously a verbal report was given to the post-partum nurse, but now days an SBAR, an acronym for Situation, Background, Assessment, and Recommendation sheet is completed and faxed to the receiving nurse. The post-partum nurses attend to all needs of the delivered patients.

The other members of our maternal child team are the nurses and pediatricians of the newborn nursery. An hour after the baby is born, the nurse and the father, or significant other take the baby to the newborn nursery for observation, assessment, Vitamin K injection and the application of Erythromycin salve to the eyes.

One of the most memorable nursery nurses was an older nurse who is now retired. She always talked to the babies as she was admitting them. She began by exclaiming "Happy Birthday, little one! My name is Maddie (not her real name) and I'm gonna take good care of you!"

The newborns stay in their mother's rooms most of the time. Routinely newborns can be discharged after forty-eight hours.

I consider every birth a miracle, but sometimes we are a part of an extraordinary story that has beaten the odds of survival. I have shared some with you. This one is the most recent.

The L&D nurses admitted the G2 P1 to the floor at twenty-one weeks gestation. She was dilated five centimeters with the amniotic membranes bulging through her cervix. Upon assessment you could actually see the baby's tiny feet through the membrane. This scenario was devastating to the young couple and so sad to the nurses. The patient was immediately placed in the Trendelenburg position and started on Magnesium Sulfate to relax her uterus. A Foley catheter was placed in her bladder and alternating leg pressure sleeves were applied around her legs to prevent blood clots. All food was held. It's a hard thing to go from a happy young mama playing with a two-year-old, to this.

The OB came in with the grim truth about her situation, but explained the possibility of doing a "rescue cerclage" if by a miracle the uterus relaxed enough that the membranes might recede reversing the dilation of the cervix where he could put a stitch in the cervix and synch it closed. The chance of a successful cerclage with a good outcome was around one percent.

The next day, the membranes had reduced decreasing the size of the cervical opening to 3 centimeters allowing a chance for the rescue cerclage. She was taken to the OR and spinal anesthesia was administered with her lying on her side. The procedure was a success. She continued to receive the Magnesium with strict bed rest. It was literally hour-to-hour for the first few days. *Would the young mother and baby remain healthy without any more labor or infection?*

Every day she held on to her baby was a step closer to a normal delivery and a healthy baby. She had many steps to go. Her husband and two-year-old were always close by. They were blessed with supportive families that stepped up the grand parenting duties. I met the couple after the worse was behind them.

She had remained in Labor and Delivery on bed rest only getting up to the bedside potty and remained on the tocolytic, Procardia, around the clock. The first thing I noticed when I entered her room was a Barbie chair. I made my way over to her and assessed her. Her husband did most everything for her. When I came in to work I made a point to pull up the chalkboard on the computer to see if she was still there. She was and he was.

I came in to work one day and she had been moved to the antepartum unit and I became her nurse every time I worked. By this time she was allowed up to the bathroom and could shower. She was another great patient, never complaining. She was not allowed wheelchair rides, but stretcher rides once a day. I got to know her family. Her daughter soon learned I'd give her ice cream and she would walk down the hall with me.

Finally, the OB gave her a target date of thirty-four weeks for discharge. We all counted down the days with her. On a Friday, around 7:15 AM the OB came in and did a cervical check announcing "no change" and she could go home a day shy of her targeted date. I've never seen a husband move so fast. He packed her bags, the toys, the Barbie chair, and their refrigerator in a flash and they were out the door. It had been an eighty-nine day hospital stay, mostly lying in a bed.

She was discharged home on bed rest and at thirty-seven weeks she was instructed to come to the office for the OB to clip the cerclage and her midwife would resume her care. At thirty-seven weeks and five days she was admitted to L&D in labor dilated six centimeters. I was working in the antepartum unit that day, but was able to attend her delivery. As I walked in during a contraction she was totally focused, composed and pushing. Shortly, baby Oliver was born at 1:07 in the afternoon, weighing seven pounds three ounces. It was an incredibly awesome delivery. (The family invites you to read about their remarkable journey at www.gshteal.blogspot.com, *The Beginning of Our Journey with Baby Oliver.*)

I absolutely love Labor and Delivery. It's my favorite. There are around twenty obstetricians, three midwives, and several family

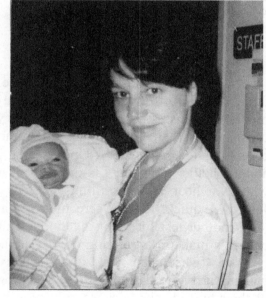

medicine residents that deliver between 250 and 300 babies each month. It requires a lot of walking, sometimes running. It's a mighty long hall from LDR one to LDR seventeen. I do it now and then, but am hobbling by the end of the shift. Now days I work most of my shifts in the six bed antepartum unit where the patient rooms are in close proximity to the nurse's station. I love it there.

Chapter Thirteen

MATERNAL CHILD HEALTH TRIAGE NURSE
2000–Present

Most all OB patients arrive as triage patients unless they are a direct admit. As soon as the nurse lays eyes on a patient the triage process begins. The main complaint we hear is "I'm having contractions" and you can have contractions without labor. The cervix changes with labor. Upon seeing a patient we have an idea about whether the patient is in labor or not. A sure sign of labor is when we hear blood curdling screams or the patient is calling, Jesus. We quickly get the screamers to Labor and Delivery.

Another test for labor is "the makeup test." It's positive if the patient's makeup is running down her face from sweat or tears. A positive "wheelchair test" means delivery is imminent. These patients arrive to the unit sitting in a wheelchair positioned on one of their butt cheeks because either the bag of water or the baby's head prevents them from sitting flat in the chair. These patients are wheeled into an LDR where they usually deliver in a matter of minutes.

For a labor check, the patients are connected to the fetal monitor, a prenatal record is obtained, and a SVE (sterile vaginal exam) is done. The patient is reassessed in an hour to check for cervical change. Preterm labor patients between twenty-five and thirty-four weeks gestation have a vaginal swab test called fetal fibronectin (FFN) which if positive, is an indicator of preterm labor. A negative result means there is little likelihood of labor within the next two weeks. They, too, are connected to the fetal monitor and have a SVE. Sometimes contractions can be stopped with IV hydration or Procardia. Up until a few years ago, if a preterm patient came in contracting we gave up to three hits of SQ (subcutaneous) Terbutaline, twenty minutes apart. It really worked well for preterm contractions. If the patient is in labor they are admitted to labor and delivery and if they are not they are discharged. Sometimes sending them home makes them mad. There are patients that come to triage two or three times complaining of contractions before they are admitted in labor.

Probably the second most common complaint we see is "I think my water broke." It is obvious on some patients, you can smell and see it. Some patients are harder to prove rupture of membranes (ROM). The fluid is tested with an amnio stick turning the swab a dark blue if positive. Sometimes the doctor or midwife does a sterile speculum exam to ascertain ROM. Vaginal secretions are swabbed and smeared on a slide then examined under a microscope. If "ferning" is present, the membranes are ruptured. Often an ultrasound is ordered to assess the amniotic fluid level or AFI. Of course, if the membranes are proved ruptured the patient is admitted.

There are many patients sent to triage with elevated blood pressures from their office visit. They are further evaluated with fetal monitoring, ultrasound, and labs. Depending on the results they are either sent home, admitted to labor and delivery, or antepartum.

Every now and then, there is a precipitous delivery in triage. We work fast *not* to let that happen. It happened to one of our own a few years back. The labor nurse came to the triage unit in active labor two days before her scheduled C-section. She was fairly composed as she breathed through her contractions. She was connected to the fetal heart monitor that showed her baby's heart rate in the eighties and her cervix was completely dilated. She pushed and little Eden was born weighing eight pounds four ounces. She holds the title of the first VBAC in our triage unit.

Scheduled C-sections come to triage for preoperative labs, paperwork, and teaching prior to the day of surgery. They are given written instructions and antiseptic scrub sponges to scrub their bellies the night before and the morning of surgery. This is proven to minimize post-operative infections. Having these preliminaries done really facilitates the flow of patients with the surgery schedule. The past few years, specified L&D nurses' work as "OR nurses" circulating the surgery cases. They are scheduled from 5 AM to 5 PM. On the day of surgery, many of the patients return to the triage unit to be readied for surgery.

Our six bed triage unit stays busy, sometimes overwhelming to me. All of the L&D nurses triage patients on weekends and holidays when the triage unit is closed. The last time I worked triage, an oriental patient came walking in as we were starting our shift. She was very quiet and stoic. Neither she nor her husband could speak or understand English. I assisted her to the stretcher and connected her to the fetal monitor while the other nurse called the language line so we could communicate with her. She was contracting, so I did a SVE, she was eight centimeters with a bulging bag of water. We whisked her to L&D where I completed her admission. Luckily, a friend came who interpreted for her. Seems like when your shift starts off a certain way it sets the tone for the whole day. Yes, it was one of those super busy days in OB triage.

Chapter Fourteen

MATERNAL CHILD HEALTH
ANTEPARTUM NURSE
2000-Present

Many patients start out in Labor and Delivery, triaged then sent home, admitted for labor, observed for twenty-four hours or admitted as antepartum patients. Many antepartum patients stayed on the L&D unit for various complications, during and after pregnancy, until our antepartum unit was opened. I've had many memorable antepartum patients. Having the same patients, often weeks at a time, we bond with them and their families.

One of the first long-term antepartum patients that I remember was a primip that I'd known since she was a teenager. It was the whole summer of 2000 that she stayed on bed rest. She was diagnosed with a complete placenta previa early on in her pregnancy. At around twenty-four weeks she was admitted to L&D with vaginal bleeding. The baby's placenta had covered her cervix, insuring that she would have a C-section when she delivered. When stabilized she was transferred to post-partum where she continued strict bed rest, periodic ultrasounds, and intermittent fetal monitoring. During the twelve weeks she was in the hospital prior to her delivery, she was brought back to the L&D periodically when vaginal bleeding occurred. During the times when she wasn't bleeding she was allowed to take a weekly shower.

The nurses pushed her in her bed to the mezzanine to attend her baby shower. At thirty-five weeks her OB did an amniocentesis for lung maturity. The baby's lungs were not mature so her cesarean section was postponed until thirty-six weeks. I stayed over that morning to help with her 7:30 AM C-section. Little Jade was born at 7:35 AM, weighing five pounds five ounces. She did well and was discharged home with her mother and daddy. *Can you imagine staying in the hospital twelve weeks prior to delivery then not being able to take your baby home with you?* That three month sacrifice really paid off. I never heard her complain. She told me later that she had bonded with many of the nurses and it was a bitter sweet good-bye when she left.

Some of the antepartum patients were post delivered on Magnesium Sulfate for the treatment of toxemia of pregnancy. My patient's Magnesium had been discontinued earlier in the day, but she was kept in L&D for close monitoring. I remember sitting with her watching Friday Night Football Fever to hear some of the high school scores. She had no complaints and seemed fine, talking and laughing. A little later I was called to her room. I went in and found her sitting straight up in bed, complaining of shortness of breath. As I began to assess her she began struggling to breathe and started coughing up pink, frothy sputum. Her oxygen saturation was down, and she was getting anxious. She was in pulmonary edema. The doctor arrived and she was quickly transferred to ICU where she was treated and the problem was resolved. It was impressive. It happened so fast.

For some unknown reason, sometimes the amniotic membranes rupture before the baby is term. We call this preterm premature rupture of membranes, PPROM. It may occur prematurely due to an infection, but sometimes nobody really knows why. I remember admitting a twenty-five week primip to L&D with gross rupture of membranes. She was out walking her dog when her water broke; it just happened. She became very sick with an infection known as chorio, short for chorioamnionitis. She received steroids, and antibiotics, but the infection were too much for the small baby.

The next week, I admitted another twenty-five week primip

with PPROM. I couldn't believe this could happen again, so soon. I was afraid of the same outcome for the young couple. Before I went into her room I had to compose myself to keep from crying. She too was treated with steroids and antibiotics. We kept a close watch for any signs of infection.

Each day the water leaked, but the mama and the baby remained healthy. After the OB thought she was stable enough she was moved to the post-partum floor where she received ultrasounds and fetal heart monitoring. On the tenth day after her water broke, some ladies came from one of the churches to pray for her. She did not know any of them. They hand made a blanket with each of their names embroidered on it with a cross in the center. They laid this blanket over her abdomen, prayed, and anointed her with oil. After this experience, her amniotic fluid began to increase until it reached a normal AFI or amniotic fluid index. This was an extraordinary thing for her membranes to reseal. I may have heard of it happening to one other patient.

At thirty weeks she was discharged home. I'd become attached to the couple, checking on her often on post-partum and at home. At thirty-six weeks, the wait was over; the OB brought her in for Cytotec placement with Pitocin induction. It was a long day for everybody, but her cervix just wasn't ripe and would not change. We took her back for a C-section and in minutes we were holding the baby girl. I wrote her story and gave it to her mama and daddy to give to her when she was old enough to understand it. Emma Jane came to see me last summer while I was on duty during a visit to Alabama. She's a smart and beautiful little girl.

THE MIRACLE OF EMMA JANE
March 29, 2004

I met you when you were twenty-five gestational weeks old at the hospital where I work. The bag of water that protected you had broken. This water bag where you lived and played, kept bad germs away and protected you from bumping your head. This was a scary time for your mama and daddy. Many times when this happens, babies are born prematurely and this is not good. Babies born this

157

early do not do well living on the outside. Their lungs can't breathe and they can't eat. The doctors and nurses did many things to your mama to keep you inside. Some of the medicine made her very sick. She had to stay in bed and could not get up for anything! You were connected to a fetal heart monitor so we could watch your heart beat and look for any problems.

Day by day, the doctors and nurses looked after you and your mama. We checked for signs of infection that could make you come early. Each day your water leaked down lower and lower. A special machine called an ultrasound measured your water level two or three times a week. Then one day, the hole in your bag of water sealed itself and there was no more leaking. We were all very happy!

Even though the water stopped leaking and your water level went up, your mama had to stay in the hospital for five weeks. She lay in the bed night and day. Then one day the doctor came in and told her she could take a shower. She was so excited! Your daddy tried to make her room like home. Her second grade class sent pictures and he hung them on the wall. Friends and family came to visit and brought all kinds of flowers and presents. This was a very hard time for your mama. She had been a very busy woman and now she was confined to a hospital room. Every day the nursed checked your by monitoring your heart beat. We could tell if you were staying healthy. You continued to have ultrasounds each week to check you and your water. You see this was very unusual that your bag of water sealed and you were doing so well!

Finally, at thirty weeks old, the doctor came in and said your mama could go home. She went home, but could not do anything but eat, sleep, shower and lay on the sofa. She was "so bored", but did exactly what the doctor said. Home nurses came to your house to check on you and your mama every day. On Mondays and Thursdays she went to her doctor's office for a checkup and ultrasound. Sometimes on the ultrasound your mama and daddy could see you sucking your thumb and you would hide your face. Every week they watched you grow!

One day when your mama was at the doctor's office, he scheduled you to be born on March 29th. You would be thirty-six weeks and three days old. All of your family made arrangements to come to the hospital on that day. Everyone was very anxious and excited. Your mama came in the afternoon before and we gave her some medicine to get her ready for your birth. The next morning we gave her special medicine to make her go into labor so you could be born. She labored all day and by 9:30 that night her labor had stopped progressing. We could tell that you were getting tired by watching the fetal monitor tracing. The doctor came in and decided you would be born by Cesarean Section. A Cesarean Section is where a baby is born through an incision in the mother's abdomen. At 10:15 PM we rolled your mama to the operating room and at 10:28 PM you were born. You came to the outside crying. The doctor handed you to me and I laid you on the warming bed. I dried you and gave you a little oxygen to make you turn pink. You were very alert. I foot printed you for the birth certificate and put your identification bands on your arm and leg. Then I wrapped you up like a burrito and put a stocking cap on your head. All we could see was your sweet little face. I took you over to your mama and daddy and laid you by your mama's face. They were so proud and happy. Your eyes were wide open as you looked around. Your daddy took you to the nursery where they weighed and measured you.

You weighed six pounds and were nineteen inches long. Your grandparents and great grandmother were outside the widow watching as the nurse gave you a shot and put medicine in your eyes. You turned your head to look at your family as you lay on the warming bed.

As I left the nursery, I thought, she is finally here, the tiny miracle, the answer to our prayers. God bless you always, sweet Emma Jane!

Camille Foshee-Mason RN

There are many, preterm labor patients admitted to L&D, and then transferred to antepartum. The doctors take into consideration gestational age, risk factors, ultrasound findings and the fetal monitor strip as to their plan of care. Many patients in preterm labor are given intravenous Magnesium Sulfate to stop labor. Due to the sedative effects of this drug patients are assessed closely for respiratory depression. They can easily get Magnesium toxicity, so blood levels are obtained every six hours. The nurses monitor hourly urine output usually from a Foley catheter, assess breath sounds and deep tendon reflexes or DTRs. If the patient's gestational age is less than thirty-four weeks, they are given a steroid injection to enhance lung maturity of the fetus. Two IM Celestone injections are given usually twenty-four hours apart. The steroid window begins forty-eight hours after the first dose. The OBs and nurses try to hold off delivery until the baby is "in the steroid window" allowing the baby less NICU days and sometimes giving them a chance at survival.

Occasionally, the OBs add Indocin to the patient's regimen of tocolytics. After a couple of days of Magnesium, preterm patients were given Brethine to manage preterm labor. The Brethine or Terbutaline was taken by mouth around the clock at home or at the hospital. An obstetrical home health nurse managed T- pumps when patients required continuous Terbutaline therapy to control contractions. The medicine was administered subcutaneously with a small needle that was placed in the mother's thigh. After 2011, Terbutaline was contraindicated in the use of preterm labor by the

FDA. Procardia, has taken its place. It seems to work well in our antepartum unit. Patients take it by mouth around the clock. You just never know how it's going to go with preterm patients. Some we think might go into labor at any time are discharged and carry their babies until term. Others have contractions and some go into labor.

One of my recent long-term pre-termers was admitted to the antepartum unit, contracting, at twenty-seven weeks, with a closed, but thin cervix. She had a history of preterm labor and delivery at twenty-eight weeks with her first baby and it looked as if this might happen again. We started a forty-eight hour Magnesium drip and gave the first of two steroid injections. Upon discontinuing the Magnesium she was started on Procardia every four hours. She was very compliant with the doctor's orders as she lived in fear of another Mag drip. At twenty-nine weeks she was allowed home on Procardia and bed rest. She was readmitted to the antepartum unit five days later, contracting, one hundred percent effaced and one centimeter dilated. She bought herself another round of Magnesium.

After three weeks of Procardia and strict bed rest she was discharged at thirty-four weeks. I received updates from her periodically as she anticipated her labor. At thirty-six weeks, she was ready to have this baby. She returned to her normal activities, posting a picture of herself in Target. Still no labor. At thirty-seven weeks her water broke and once again she was admitted, but this time to L&D. Andrew was born weighing six pounds eleven ounces.

When she was discharged home, little Andrew was discharged with her. Their sacrifices paid off.

Andrew's parents are a military couple with a three-year-old and like many military families they had no family in town. The husband had to juggle his job, mommy duties, and daddy duties. I have the utmost respect for the military couples. It's an honor to attend to them.

How wonderful it is to have multiples, but how hard it is to avoid an antepartum stay with them? I would say all triplet mothers spend some time in antepartum and many twin mothers are admitted there as well. Whether, single, twin, or triplet gestation, preterm labor is treated the same.

In the last couple of years we've seen more patients admitted with a diagnosis of a short cervix. This is usually found in the doctor's office with a SVE and ultrasound. These patients are kept on bed rest in antepartum, sometimes for weeks.

My most memorable short cervix story involved a wonderful couple expecting twins. The young primip was sent from the office to antepartum at twenty-two weeks. She had a positive FFN test and was administered Magnesium Sulfate, steroids, and antibiotics upon admission. Twenty-two weeks is mighty early and honestly I feared the worst for her. After Magnesium she was given Procardia around the clock. As she stabilized, she was given bathroom privileges and finally allowed to take a quick shower every other day. She and her husband had the best attitude and her motto was, "I'll do what I have to do." She never complained and spent many hours on her computer during her stay. Her husband was at her side after work and weekends sleeping on one of our portable cots. At thirty-four weeks she was discharged home with obstetrical home services for monitoring and assessment. I was working in the recovery room the day she was admitted in labor. She was taken into the OR to deliver her thirty-five week twins. I was asked to assist in a twin delivery and what a wonderful surprise to see who it was—a couple I knew well. Little Kelsea was born first weighing four pounds five ounces, followed by her brother, Nicholas, weighing in at four pounds eight ounces. Nicholas was discharged with his mama while Kelsea stayed a week in the NICU. I've watched them grow on the social media, perfect, beautiful, children.

I had another twin patient in antepartum with a similar story. She was sent to The University of Alabama Medical Center in Birmingham during her pregnancy where they fitted her with a pessary to minimize pressure on her cervix from the weight of twins and a pregnant uterus; a new use for an old device.

There are many young pregnant women with high blood pressure. Some have chronic hypertension and take daily medication to control it, others get it with pregnancy. We admit both to the antepartum for close observation of the mother and the baby. It is unbelievable how much blood pressure medicine some of these women take. I've had patients on all three of the most prescribed medications used during pregnancy, Procardia, Labetalol and Aldomet. They continue to run blood pressures in the 140/80s.

We monitor their blood pressures, obtain 24-hour urines for protein, draw labs, and look for signs and symptoms of preeclampsia. We assess the babies with ultrasound scans to assess the growth, amniotic fluid, and movement of the babies. A reassuring non-stress test on the fetal heart monitor is a positive sign that the baby is okay. These women seem to get sick so fast. When that happens they are started on Magnesium Sulfate to prevent seizures and are delivered. Many of the patients are brought back to the antepartum and kept on Magnesium for twenty-four hours after delivery. We have a protocol for Mag Sulfate whether it's used in PTL (pre-term labor) or preeclampsia. As these new mothers begin to diuresis, their blood pressures come down. Some of them remain hypertensive and are discharged on blood pressure medications. There are patients that have been home a few days and return to be admitted with post-partum preeclampsia. They, too, are treated with Magnesium and intravenous blood pressure medications. Seems like we see more of it these days. I wonder if preeclampsia is more prevalent here in the South.

Uncontrolled diabetics—whether gestational, Type I or Type II—are admitted to our unit. We try to control what they eat and monitor their blood sugars. There are some patients that control their diabetes with blood sugars and an insulin pump. Even knowledgeable and compliant patients have to have a Snickers bar at times. We become diabetic educators as part of our nursing duties. Some patients will comply under our watchful eye, but return to noncompliance when they leave the hospital. Diabetic mothers have big babies, a condition which is known as macrosomia.

It's been my observations that if a woman has gallstones or kidney stones lurking in her body, they'll surface while she's pregnant. With either kind of stone, the patient usually arrives writhing in pain with her head in a basin nauseated and vomiting. We hydrate them and administer intravenous medication for the pain and nausea. Renal or gallbladder ultrasounds are done. We strain urine and keep and I&O on the kidney stone patients. Usually there's a urology consult for a kidney stone. If they're lucky the stone passes and the pain resolves. Sometimes patients have to have a stent placed in their ureter to keep the urine from backing up in the kidney. If gallstones are diagnosed, a surgeon is called to consult. Many times the gallstone patients are delivered prior to term, and then undergo a lap cholecystectomy.

Pregnant women in their second trimester with Pyelonephritis are sometimes admitted to the antepartum unit. I've witnessed how quickly they can get sick. A twenty-five week primip was admitted to post-partum with pyelonephritis, with a fever of 103 degrees. She was transferred to antepartum the next day, with high fever, tachypnea, and low oxygen saturation. She didn't look good and I had a bad feeling about her. Her OB came and assessed her as she made a turn for the worse. She was taken to the OR for an emergency C-section, then straight to the ICU for mechanical ventilation. She had gone into Adult Respiratory Distress Syndrome, or ARDS. She did recovery from this illness. One thing that complicated this scenario was that she spoke and understood little English.

I first heard about pica foods when I studied OB in nursing school. Pica foods are ice, clay, sand, and starch, to name a few. They have no nutritional value. I'd seen some homemade packaged nuggets of white clay on the counters of convenience stores, thinking to myself; *do people really eat that?* Yes, they do. I've seen clay and starch in a few antepartum patients' rooms. The patients were embarrassed when I brought attention to it.

Occasionally, a nurse would be needed to go with a patient on a transfer to Birmingham. Can you believe I actually volunteer to ride in an ambulance? Yes, I've accompanied several patients on transfers and without incidence. I ride with those severe pre-eclamptic patients that could seize at any bump in the road managing their Magnesium infusion.

In the spring of 2012, came my third computer challenge. All doctor's orders were to be entered into the computer and the nurses had to learn it also. This new computerized physician order entry is known as C-POE. All hospitals across the nation are transitioning to it. It's the same computer system that was there when I was hired, but I'd never used it. One of the techs always did it for me. Now, I had to bite the bullet and learn it. I didn't even know my password. The big news was the system was "going live" in June. I didn't even know what that meant.

We had all these computer gurus that came from all around the country to teach us. In the class I went to, there was this young nurse that sat by me. She was from the neuroscience floor of our sister hospital. I tried to keep up with the instructor as they clicked from this to that. If I was hesitant, she'd reach over and show me where to click. So today, I can do most of it, only asking for a little assistance now and then.

I was working in the antepartum unit last year when I received a phone call from one of the OBs. He said he was sending over a patient who was carrying "a miracle baby." The first thing that ran through my head was he's sending over a fifty-year-old woman having her first baby. That wasn't the case, but, yes, indeed this was a "miracle baby."

The G4P3 had a history of two previous C-sections and a hospitalization at fifteen weeks with this pregnancy with a diagnosis of abdominal pain and hemorrhaging. She underwent exploratory surgery discovering a live fetus with part of its placenta growing through her old C-section scar. This life threatening diagnosis is known as a placenta percreta.

The OB removed that part of the placenta and repaired the uterus. I didn't even know that could be done. The patient showed concern of some spotting at her OB appointment so she was admitted at twenty-five weeks and two days gestation. We watched her closely as she progressed, assessing the fetus and her uterus with daily non-stress test and weekly ultrasounds. She remained on bed rest with occasional wheelchair rides for sixty-four days. Because she was such a high risk patient and needed IV access a PICC line was inserted which we flushed daily and changed the dressing every Wednesday.

A C-section was scheduled at thirty-four weeks and two days. As the date drew near, the nurses got a little antsy worrying about things that could happen. She was totally confident in her doctor and never appeared anxious or worried. We kept her in our prayers as the morning finally arrived. It all went well and the little "miracle baby" arrived weighing six pounds eleven ounces. They named him Joseph. After only a week in the NICU he was discharged home with his parents and three sisters.

Our six bed antepartum stays full and busy, sometimes overflowing into Labor and Delivery. It's staffed with two RNs. We receive a verbal and typed report from the night shift. Many patients require continuous fetal monitoring and others receive non-stress test once or twice a day. Upon admission, patients' labs are drawn and IV access, or INT, and placed and changed every three days. Consents for delivery and blood products are obtained. The admission assessment is done, and the plan of care initiated. A type and screen for blood is kept current requiring a venipuncture every seventy-two hours. We assist the patients with baths and provide linen changes. Some of the patients require bed baths which includes washing their hair with a water pitcher and a trash can. Some of us give pedicures. Bedbound patients wear alternating pressure devices on their legs and some receive Lovenox injections to prevent DVTs. In the last few months, some of the doctors have been ordering the injection Makena, a hormone progestin. It is given to pregnant women who have had history of premature delivery. We give the medicine intramuscularly once a week. Back in the day we gave the same medicine under the name Delalutin.

The nurses educate patients on their specific problems or diagnosis and discuss their plan of care with them. The NICU doctors and nurses are in close contact with us keeping abreast of possible admissions to the NICU. They are very good to come and talk to the preterm mothers. The lactation nurses assist the delivered patients with breast feeding or pumping if their babies are in the NICU. We try to accommodate our patients and make their stay in our unit as best as possible. We are constantly admitting, discharging, and transferring patients in and out of antepartum.

Most all of our patients bring in computers, IPODs, books, needlework and about anything to pass the time while on bed rest. If they are told they'll probably be there for weeks, some haul in big screen TVs and small refrigerators. Some rooms have so many electronics we have to be careful to not trip over a cord.

If patients happen to be there at Christmas, many of the families bring in small Christmas trees and the holiday is celebrated in their rooms. Baby showers are also held in these antepartum room with friends coming and going leaving gifts and good wishes. We try to allow patients to have some control of their schedules, such as sleeping late in the mornings or eating at odd hours. It's hard to stay in one room for days, weeks, and even months. Most of them do not complain and have an attitude of "doing all I can for my baby." The most frequently asked question I hear from the patients and their families is, "when do you think I will have my baby?"

My response is the same, "I don't have a crystal ball you need to relax and take one day at a time." I tell them I understand it is hard to leave their families, but that they are where they need to be for now.

Chapter Fifteen

LUCKY LILY

As a nurse and grandmother, my girls usually call me with minor ailments or injuries with their children. I give them my opinion on what to do and whether the child needs to been seen by a doctor.

On Monday night February 23rd, 2009, I got a call from my youngest daughter saying that her two year old was climbing up the drawers of a night stand that turned over pulling a nineteen inch TV down hitting her head. I quickly dropped what I was doing and drove to their house. Little Lily was sitting in her mama's lap with a huge purple "goose egg" right above her left eye. Trying to keep it together, I told her parents we needed to get her to the emergency room now.

She was seen immediately at our community hospital and whisked to the CT room. The ER doctor knew me and within minutes showed me her film on the PAX right outside of her room. She had a skull fracture and he pointed out a small bone fragment that was not connected to anything, I could see it so clearly. He told us that arrangements were being made to transfer her to Children's Hospital in Birmingham and shortly I heard the helicopter landing. The flight team, included a flight nurse and paramedic rushed in as the ER nurses readied her for transport. I had to take a minute so I slipped out the familiar backdoor of the hospital. There it was, the Air Evac.

A man wearing a jumpsuit was standing a few feet away. I thought to myself that must be the pilot. He was an older stocky man, probably a Vietnam veteran. The next thing I knew the nurses were wheeling Lily out on a stretcher to the helicopter.

I got as close as I could and asked "Can I ride with her, I'm a nurse and her grandmother?"

"No ma'am," they replied. "There's no room."

That transport helicopter was very impressive. Every little bit of space was utilized in caring for the patient. They secured her to the helicopter and connected the cables to monitor her vital signs. She of course had an IV line to administer any necessary drugs.

As far as her vital signs, she was stable and she had not lost consciousness. She wasn't crying. My daughter and son-in law left directly from the hospital driving to Birmingham. The pilot started the engine and the huge blades whirled faster and faster until it lifted from the ground. I watched them fly out of sight. These were the worse minutes of my entire life.

She and the flight team made it safely to Children's, landing on a helipad on the roof of the hospital. She was taken to an exam room in the Emergency Department for evaluation with the neurosurgeon on call. I drove the two hour trip alone praying and talking to God. Like most accidents, it happened so quickly. She had a lot going for her and I tried to stay positive. She was admitted to the Pediatric Intensive Care Unit. Inside the PICU, children of all ages were in cribs or beds lined up perpendicular to the walls. We were allowed to visit two at a time. Our little Lily seemed stable and conscious as the area around her left eye became more swollen and discolored. She slept at intervals while connected to monitors displaying her vital signs. We took turns rocking her at the bedside. Many specialists with their entourages evaluated her. She had a left orbit fracture and the bone fragment seemed to be the big concern as to whether or not to operate on her. There was a possibility of that fragment piercing the dura setting up an infection. The dura mater or dura is a thick membrane that protects the brain and spinal cord. The nurses in the PICU were young and very good. They took good care of her. One of the nurses told us that TV accidents are fairly common and not all children with this kind of accident are as lucky as Lily. The PICU nurses gave her the nickname "Lucky Lily" and by discharge doctors and nurses called her that.

After two days in the PICU waiting room, we heard other children's stories and we felt very fortunate. Some were so heartbreaking. We saw parents sleeping in the waiting room that had been there for weeks. Lily was transferred to the neuro floor on Wednesday awaiting surgery to repair the fracture Friday morning. She was a good little patient watching hours of Barney. She was allowed to ride in a wagon around the hospital. She pointed and commented on the many colorful cows that were located throughout the common areas. Each time Lily was on the neuro floor, she was assigned to Maria, (not her real name) RN. Lily and the rest of us quickly bonded with Maria and found comfort in her experience and knowledge, for she had worked there many years. She not only gave great care to Lily, but took time to explain things and answer questions.

Friday morning, we kissed our baby girl "good-bye" as they took her to the OR. Many family and friends gathered in the surgery waiting room and within an hour the surgeon came out with a good report. The fracture was repaired and she should be fine. I was the only person that asked questions. After surgery, she was taken back to the PICU for twenty-four hours then she returned to the neuro floor under the care of Maria until her discharge on Monday.

I hope none of you ever have to experience any sort of accident with a family member. Lily's mama and daddy never left the hospital and stayed by her side as much as was permitted. The support of her family and friends was unbelievable. Lily had so many Mylar balloons the ceiling was covered, no latex balloons were permitted. The folks in our small town brought gifts, food, and money to the family. I came home a couple of days after the accident. As I drove through town there was a marque that said "Pray for Lily." Lucky Lily recovered and today she's perfect.

A few weeks after her surgery, out of the blue, Lily walked into the kitchen and asked her Mama, "Why is Jesus in my room?" I suppose He came to check on her.

Chapter Sixteen

SBAR

I don't know if I chose nursing or if nursing chose me. Maybe I was *called* to be a nurse. I can honestly say I've always loved nursing. If I had it to do all over, I would do it again. The rewards have been too great to change anything. I was content with whatever nursing specialty I was doing and never considered going back to school. I've been a part of and witnessed many changes in nursing over the past forty years.

Certainly the most obvious change is our appearance. Gone are the white uniforms, caps, and white shoes. Really nobody knows who we are unless they read our badge or we are introduced to them. Today nurses wear any color scrubs and funky shoes. Jewelry seems to be allowed and most hair styles are accepted. I haven't seen a nurse with pink or purple hair at my hospital, but it's probably permitted in some places. After I went to the city hospital to work, while walking to the cafeteria one day, I saw a woman walking tall, urgently down the hall. As she got closer, I could see she was wearing a crisp white uniform, a cap, and white shoes. I wanted to jump up and down cheering as she walked by. For sure you could pick her out in a crowd.

Even though I had three male students in my graduating class, I don't recall any male nurses that worked at the hospital where I did my training. They, too, wore white uniforms "back in the day," but have transformed into different colored scrubs.

When I was in training we addressed one another with Mr., Mrs., or Miss. I've continued this practice over the year. I was raised to address my elders in this way, instead of addressing strangers only by their first name. Nurses refer to one another by their first names. Today, only doctors and some patients have a prefix before their names. Even though many of the doctors are way younger than me, I answer with a "Yes, ma'am, or Yes, sir." I don't stand just because a doctor is present. I let that rule go many years ago. But if there is no empty chair at the desk and they want to sit, I give them mine.

There has been some changes in bedside nursing, meaning there are monitors and machines that do some of the work for us, such as vital signs. If I had a nickel for every manual blood pressure I've taken, I'd be rich.

I continue to be very particular when working the recovery room or PACU. Even though patients may have a family member at the bedside, sitting up, talking, and the monitors show perfect vital signs, I like to stay right at the bedside. I don't even like to step away to get something. Our instructors really hammered that *one* in.

Whether at the bedside or at the nurse's desk most all of our charting is done on the computer. The young nurses learn it very quickly and are very fast since they are computer natives. Some are tolerant of us older nurses when we ask questions and are patient when explaining a new screen; some are not. I know which ones to ask. One day I was at the L&D desk checking my calls on my new I-phone with the younger nurses around.

One exclaimed "Oh, Camille, *you* have an I-phone?"

Another one chimed in. "Do you know how to use it?"

I replied, "I'm learning."

∾

In today's world, state board exams are known as the NCLEX and they are taken on computer. The new graduates know their results in a few days. Even my licensure has changed over the years. Before online capabilities we filled out the renewal application by hand, added a money order, and mailed it back to the Board of Nursing. Years later we had to list our Continuing

Education Units on the renewal application. Today, we access the Board of Nursing online, complete the information, and type in a credit card number. My CEUs are sent to the board from my employer. I pay seventy-five dollars every other year to renew my license.

For the last couple of years our time is done on e-time on the computer. We clock in and out on the e-time screen accessing it with a login and password.

Nurses have to keep up with new technology. The evolution of nursing has revolved around technology as you can see from previous chapters. One of the latest pieces of equipment that I've seen, is a vein scanner used on patients that are difficult sticks. One of the ED nurses brought it to L&D for us to see. We placed our hands and forearms under the scanner visualizing our veins that looked like a road map.

During my career I've worked around many remarkable nurse anesthetists, or CRNAs. I remember back in the seventies and early eighties watching them work. They were all women and were in constant motion as they attended their patients. I don't think there were any monitors. All vital signs were done manually while intermittently squeezing the anesthesia bag and pushing the IV medications. The nurse anesthetist had an ear piece she wore so she could hear the heartbeat, respirations, and the blood pressure of the patient. This earpiece was connected to two stethoscopes enabling her to assess vital signs as she charted them on the anesthesia flow sheet. When the OR table had to be positioned to facilitate the operation, the nurse anesthetist had to manually crank the table. I recently saw general anesthesia administered to a patient. The patient was connected to all sorts of monitors, and ventilations were maintained by a machine. If the surgeon needed the table repositioned, the CRNA simply maneuvered it with a button.

I've seen the latest and greatest in the operating room, the Da Vinci robot. It's astounding. The surgeon sat about eight feet away from the patient at a console where he maneuvered the arms and hands of the robot. The wrists of the robot could turn at any angle working in hard-to-get places as the instruments clamped, cauterized, and sutured tissue. I sat at the head of the bed with one of my CRNA friends as I watched the operation on a big screen. It was so precise and defined. The surgeon spoke through a microphone communicating with the scrub nurses and techs. Not only do the surgeons master these new surgical options, but the OR nurses and scrub techs also stay abreast with new surgical technology. As I've said before, I could never be an OR nurse.

One day I was thumbing through a Med-Surg textbook that was left in antepartum by the new graduates. In the text it referred to the patients as clients. *Really?* I'll continue to call them *patients.*

Another obvious change in nursing care is with the patients themselves. Look around, many of them are bigger. Obesity is a vast health problem in our country today. Obesity can lead to diabetes and hypertension. At the community hospital, we had one over-sized wheelchair that was kept in the ER. Most patients rode in a standard size wheelchair with transporting, admissions and discharges. Today, it's the exact opposite. Our L&D unit is equipped with oversized wheelchairs. A label reads Maximum capacity 500 pounds. I think there's one standard size wheelchair in the fleet. Sad but true. As nurses, it's more difficult to transfer, reposition, and care for heavier patients whether it's a labor patient with an epidural or a stroke patient. It's sad to see these young women being admitted to our unit weighing close to 300 pounds. After delivery when they're so happy, I hate to bring up the weight issue and most of the time I don't. Imagine what's down the road for them when they reach forty if they don't change their habits.

The diet of patients is another change which is the main reason for the aforementioned. *How much pizza and fried chicken can folks eat?* Many patients don't eat the hospital food provided, but have food brought in from fast food restaurants. Back in the day, if food was brought to the hospital it was a home cooked meal brought in on a plate covered with foil. It was usually vegetables with little meat. There were no microwaves. The reason it was even brought to the hospital was because the patient wouldn't eat for one reason or another.

On our admission record we list the number and whereabouts of tattoos and piercings that patients have. Most all of our patients have their ears pierced and if they have other piercings, I ask them to remove them. I've seen piercings just about everywhere. Back in the seventies and eighties, if I saw a tattoo on a patient, it was more likely on a man that had been in the service.

I recall one of our OB patients having a rather large black

widow spider tattooed on her pregnant belly. The California OB and nurses called her "the black widow." Now, just about all of the young mamas have at least one tattoo. If a tattoo happens to be in the C-section incision the OB puts it back together perfectly.

Some of our young mothers have a cell phone glued to their ear. After asking them nicely, sometimes I have to say, "I need to ask you some questions and do an assessment so I need for you to get off your phone." Some become offended when asked to lay down their phone.

We are mindful of those patients with latex allergies. Each unit has a latex free cart that holds all of the needed supplies. Our exam gloves and many other patient care supplies are latex free.

Back in the late eighties, nurses began to educate patients on their illnesses and medications usually with discharge. Home health patients received verbal and written instructions that were left in a folder in their homes. Today, patient education is a large part of our job. Upon admission teaching begins and continues throughout the hospital stay. Some of today's patients take the initiative and educate themselves about their illness or surgeries using the internet. The well-informed patient asks questions and is usually compliant with medications and instructions.

In 1996, HIPAA, or Health Insurance Portability and Accountability Act was passed mandating rules and regulations including patient privacy and confidentiality. We were instructed on these new laws and have become mindful and compliant with them. Over the past eighteen years the HIPPA laws have transitioned from hard charts to computer charts. Therefore this mandate includes, faxing, texting, and the social medias.

With OSHAs Bloodborne Pathogens and Needlestick Safety and Prevention Act of 2000 there became a heighten awareness to bloodborne pathogens and diseases. We'd become accustomed to sharps containers and disposable gloves being readily available. We were introduced to "safety needles." I'll be honest, the first time I had to give an IM injection with one of them, I thought I'd stick myself. Those needles have taken some time to get used to. From the beginning, I really liked the needleless IV tubing and secondary sets. I am thankful to individuals and companies that have devised and perfected items that have made our jobs safer. In the past, I didn't give much thought about contracting any illness except the stomach virus. I wear gloves most every time I do patient care even a linen change. Times have certainly changed.

It's sad to say, but we are more mindful of safety for patients and ourselves than we were in the past. I have a badge with my picture on it that I scan to get through doors and into units of the hospital. We have a security system for our newborns. Years ago there were only two warnings; Code Black for tornadoes and a Code Red for fire. Today, we have a code for every possible kind of threat to our patients and employees. Security guards walk the halls and respond quickly if needed. Metal detectors are set up at public entrances to many hospitals, especially Emergency Departments. Security constantly monitors the parking lots.

In 2011, our hospital and other ones became smokeless facilities. No one, patients or employees, smoked in the building or on the grounds. However, there are some that sit in their cars or walk off the grounds to smoke.

Whenever I order labs or medications on the computer, it reminds me how far medicine has come. In the early days, a CBC (Complete Blood Count) and chemistry were the main labs ordered. Now, there's a lab test for most anything in question. There are so many medications these days—its mind boggling.

Surgical advancements such as laparoscopies and robotics have allowed the patients much shorter length of hospital stays, fewer traumas to their bodies, and decreased pain. It's amazing when I compare post-op patients from my training days to now.

This is only one example, a thoracotomy. To remove the lower lobe of a lung meant days in the ICU followed by many days in the hospital. Patients had a long mean incision and a stationary chest tube. These patients were slow to ambulate (walk) increasing the risks of complications. Recently a friend of mine went into the OR on a Monday morning for removal of her lower left lobe with dissection of the lymph nodes. Remarkably she was home sitting in her recliner by Wednesday afternoon. She had four small incisions and one where the chest tube was. She took Motrin for pain when she got home.

There are many rewards that come with being a nurse, including a decent salary, flexible schedules, the ability to get a job, and benefits. Then there are the real rewards.

What compensation it is to attend the birth of a baby and watch the mama as she sees it for the first time. To see one born and transition to the outside is such an amazing experience. All births are unique, but to see one where you know the mother has sacrificed and beat the odds really makes it all worth it.

An added bonus is to see some of these babies grow up. It's a good feeling to sit at awards programs at our elementary school and hear each name called knowing I was there when some of them were born. There have been times when I have been shopping and someone exclaims, "Camille, remember me. You were my labor nurse!"

I smile and pretend I remember them, but you can't recall them all and most look different when they aren't pregnant.

I've made lasting friendships with my nursing school classmates, co-workers, and patients over the years. Age never mattered to me, and now it's easy to stay connected to people with the social media. I've gathered with my nursing classmates on three separate occasions for class reunions. We always catch up where we left off.

I see members of my former hospital family at hospital reunions, retirement parties, and unfortunately, funerals. For the past five years we've gotten together on "the Operator's" birthday as he remains fit and full of wit.

Over the years, we've overcome the fear of the gruff surgeon and look forward to his parties. His eightieth birthday was a big celebration, where we hosted over a hundred well-wishers mostly hospital employees. The party continued as the limo pulled up to the door and sixteen of us climbed aboard with the honoree for a late dinner in the city. I'd never ridden in a limousine. Powered by a gallon of margaritas and two bottles of wine, we were a lively bunch by the time we turned onto the interstate. We told stories about the old days as the doctor sat wearing a crown and a blinking badge that said, "It's my birthday." The next day my face hurt from laughing so much.

Two of my favorite co-workers were the two LPNS that took me in and showed me the ropes back in 1978. They were my "working buddies." The three of us have visited many times over the years after they retired and we've kept up with each other. The older one became my home health patient when her health deteriorated and the other one sat with her many hours when she could no longer do for herself. It was hard to see her struggle as we turned her, rubbing her skin and offered her sips of Ensure or water. She was one of the sweetest and most compassionate nurses I've ever known. Everybody loved her.

There's satisfaction in knowing that you've made a difference in someone's life. It might be something big like preventing a bad outcome. One of our triage nurses was completing a pre-op assessment and paperwork for a scheduled C-section. When listening for fetal heart tones she didn't like what she heard. She took action and that baby was quickly delivered by C-section probably saving its life.

Nurses make a difference on a smaller note. Some patient's don't ever forget the nurse that gave them pain medicine—especially for a kidney stone.

With flexible schedules that nursing offers, I rarely missed any events that my girls were involved in. Today, I am fortunate to work PRN (as needed) and I can usually work my schedule around anything in which my grandchildren participate. My co-workers and I have always helped one another by swapping days to accommodate our needs.

One of the new graduates was working in antepartum one day, when she asked, "Miss Camille, what advice can you give me as a new nurse?" I was surprised, I don't recall anybody ever asking me that. I threw out a few things to her. On the way home that night I began to think about it. This is what I came up with.

Make a good first impression, you can only do that once.
Keep your word to your patients; they'll remember if you don't.
Always do the right thing, and you won't go wrong.
Be a team player, everything works better if you are.
In a crises pray, sometimes that is the only thing you can do.
Work a year of Med-Surg after graduation to perfect your skills.
Wear support stockings, your legs will appreciate it.
Keep off excess pounds, your knees will appreciate it.
Wear shoes with good support, your feet will appreciate it.
Get under the care of a good chiropractor, your body will appreciate it.

There is one other thing worth mentioning. It's easy to get a preconceived attitude toward a patient simply by a verbal report or hearing harmful comments. If the reporting nurse rolls her eyes or says, "they're crazy," let all that go in one ear and out the other. Listen to pertinent information and delete all the negative. You never know, you may bond with that patient and they may become one of your favorite patients

In my opinion, these are the qualities of a good nurse:

Flexible. *Adapt to change. Many times it means an "instant" change in direction, such as when a labor patient becomes an emergency section or a gunshot wound is brought into the ED. Long term flexibility is when you know a change is coming, such as a new computer program. Open your mind to the change and learn it. The five most dreaded words that are said to a nurse are "I have to pull you!" After the initial, "who me?" you suck it up and go.*

Dependable. *Sometimes you have to "call in," you just can't make it. Most of us can suffer through a minor illness at work. Get to work on time and do what is expected of you. Show management and your co-workers they can count on you.*

Respectful. *Respect yourself, your patients, your co-workers, and the doctors.*

Organized. *To make your job easier, you have to "get organized." This includes prioritizing. These are duties that need to be done first. Sometimes it takes a while, but you learn from others and doing it yourself. A great charge nurse is super organized and on top of everything.*

Compassionate. *Show compassion to your patients. This is done by being sympathetic and empathetic. Try to understand what they are going through. Sometimes stop and put yourself in their place.*

Resourceful. *Make good use of your time and improvise using some ingenuity to use what you have and make it work. Save steps* *by thinking ahead gathering many supplies instead of one at a time.*

Communication Skills. *It is important to have good speaking and listening skills to communicate with whoever is involved in a conversation. Be a good listener. Whether in person or on the phone, be courteous and speak clearly. Sometimes it's good to have written notes to expedite a report to a nurse or doctor. Back in the day I could rattle off information without prompting; now I have notes in my hand.*

There are no diploma nursing schools left in Alabama. Nationwide, diploma schools have declined to less than ten percent with the schools being affiliated with universities and colleges instead of hospitals. Most of today's registered nurses graduate with an Associate Degree or a Bachelor's Degree in Nursing. Some hospitals that hire ASN nurses now require them to obtain a BSN in a specific timeframe. Many of the BSN graduates continue or return to school earning a Master's Degree in Nursing which includes, certified nurse practitioners, certified registered nurses anesthetist and certified nurse midwives. Some nurses received their degrees to become nurse educators. With online capabilities, it's much easier these days to continue their education. Today's graduate nurses have more options. They can work in hospitals, long care facilities, home health, rehabilitation, clinics, schools, occupational nursing, travel nursing, and in triage for insurance companies.

I began writing my memoir eighteen months ago. The writing, in itself, has been quite a sentimental journey. I dusted them off, and began scanning the pages of my nursing textbooks to jog my memory. I was surprised at how well I remembered the tattered pages, especially the pictures. I learned a lot during those three years and was so young to go out into the world to take care of sick people. During these months, I've talked with nurses and doctors asking questions about the way things were done years ago. I appreciate their time and interest.

Last spring, I traveled to the mill-town where I did my training meeting with two of my nursing instructors, who I haven't seen since graduation, thirty-seven years ago. I met my Med-Surg instructor at the city museum. She has worked many hours preserving our nursing heritage by collecting and displaying memorabilia of the hospital and the school of nursing. There was a manikin dressed in our uniform, pin, cap, and navy cape. She and others had put together photo albums including one that had all the graduation photos of the school in chronological order. Together we drove to one of the Baptist churches where my Fundamentals instructor headed up a soup kitchen for folks in the community. We visited over lunch. These two recalled our nursing curriculum and answered my questions. They gave updates on other instructors and many of the school's nurses. They really hadn't changed a lot, just older. Both retired, but still giving of themselves and making a difference in the lives of people in their community.

We drove across town to the medical complex. The hospital had expanded, keeping up with modern-day medical advancements. Some of the buildings were torn down and replaced with new ones. Our nursing school and dorm were still there. The pristine white building had been painted. As I stood at the foot of the steps that I had run up hundreds of times, I saw the breezeway that connected the two buildings. It was exactly the same. I walked into the dorm which now houses administrative offices of the hospital and saw the old telephone booth. Maybe they left it there as a shrine to the students that used it. *Why didn't I come back, way before now?*

On June 22nd of 2013, sixty-five of us gathered for a school of nursing reunion in the conference room inside our dorm. There were fourteen of my classmates who attended the event including the "token male" who is now eighty years old. We were the youngest class represented. As we sat together, many spoke of their careers and the changes they'd gone through. The common thread within all of us was pride and dedication; pride in our careers and who we had become, and our dedication to our profession.

∾∾

It's the Tuesday after Labor Day 2013. I'm working in the antepartum unit with an assignment of three patients. After the shift report, keeping in mind, patient acuity, I make a quick round to check on the patients, putting a face with the name. If they're awake, I introduce myself and assess the patient documenting it at the bedside computer. While doing a little housekeeping in their room, I ask if they need anything. After rounding with the doctors I enter any verbal order into the computer. I administer medications by first obtaining them from the Pyxis Med Station then scanning the patient's armbands and the individual packaged medications. I watch the fetal monitor screen if front of me, and document any pertinent information. I pause for a moment to stop and think. *Has it really been forty years since I walked into that room of potential nurses at eighteen years of age?* And here I am today.

It's sort of surreal. It went so fast. Nursing is not only what I do, but a nurse is who I am. Through the years, I've weathered the changes and the computer. I've stood in awe of medical miracles, witnessed many births, and held the hand of the dying. Today, I try to stay on course and hopefully I'll retire one day.

I snap back into reality as one of the young nurses stops in to catch up on some charting at one of the desktop computers. She quickly turns and looks at me and says, "Oh, Camille, I love your new shoes."

I look down at my hot pink Crocs and reply, "Thanks, girl, I love 'em too."

Gathering of nurse, aides, and unit secretaries from our community hospital

June 1976 Class of '76

Summer of 1981 Fifth Year Reunion

1996, 20th Class Reunion

June 2013 Class Reunion

Chapter Seventeen

THE NURSE CURSE

My definition of the nurse curse is a weirdness or misfortune that happens to nurses when they are a patient. The term is frequently used in our unit by the doctors and nurses. I did a little survey asking doctors. "Do you acknowledge the nurse curse?" Eighty-five per cent said they did.

These are their stories.

My name is Melissa, RN. I am a Labor and Delivery Nurse and I have the curse. My husband and I were married thirteen years before deciding to have a baby. I'd worked on the unit two years and at thirty-three years old felt it was now, or never. I had no difficulty getting pregnant. I had a great pregnancy except for some swelling of my feet and legs. I continued to wear my wedding rings and regular scrubs only gaining twenty-seven pounds the entire pregnancy. I worked until I was thirty-seven weeks and at that time I had an ultrasound showing my son weighed eight pounds. I was scheduled for an induction of labor the next week. It was a

Wednesday afternoon when I was admitted. My doctor checked my cervix. It was closed, thick, and high. He placed 50 micrograms of Cytotec vaginally hoping it would ripen my cervix and be more conducive to the Pitocin. I asked him to order the fifty "mics" doses and received 2 more doses of the 50 microgram orally. I wanted to have no doubts if I ended up in with a C-section.

My doctor came in the next morning to break my water, but was unable to do so because my cervix had not changed even with the Pitocin on thirty. My back was hurting pretty bad, so my nurse suggested that I take some Stadol and Phenergan to relax me and maybe I would dilate. The medication knocked me out for three hours. The vaginal exam at lunch time was still the same so we discussed the options of a C-section or a two-day induction. I bought a little more time with a decision to be rechecked at 4 PM and if there was no change to proceed with the C-section. Well, by 3 PM my back was killing me. I asked the nurse to stop the Pitocin and if my cervix hadn't changed to call the doctor and go with a C-section.

My beautiful baby boy was born at 4:44 PM on Thursday Sept. 30, 2004 with some of my nurse friends in attendance. I began to feel really sick after he was born. After I saw him for a minute, I remember thinking, "Okay, I've seen my baby and now I'm going to die."

I told the CRNA that I was nauseated as I saw my heart rate on the monitor at forty-two bpm (beats per minute). I could hear them talking about excess bleeding and I wasn't surprised because I had been on Pitocin for many hours and my uterus was exhausted. The CRNA gave me Methergine, Torodol and Zofran, so I began to feel better, but every time the blood pressure cycled my hand would spasm in a clonic-tonic manner. This continued into the Recovery Room until the anesthesiologist gave me some Calcium Gluconate which stopped the spasms immediately. I remember thinking, "that was my bad luck."

My post-partum stay was fairly normal except I was so thirsty and I noticed I had increased swelling. I had no signs and symptoms of a 6/20 H&H so I was discharged with a prescription of iron. I thought I had lost some weight; after all I had a nine pound three ounce baby. I'd lost no weight.

My first night home I slept in a recliner. I had a terrible

headache on Monday and returned to the OB triage unit for PIH labs with by blood pressures in the 149/90 range. My labs were "okay."

The next day at my doctor's appointment he removed my staples and told me my headaches were most likely from my anemia. The rest of the week, I continued with the swelling and was unable to lie in my bed to sleep. Every time I lay my head back, I felt like I was suffocating. I thought I was having a PE (pulmonary emboli), but I'd convinced myself I knew too much and I was having a panic attack. I knew sometimes it took weeks for the swelling to resolve so I continued on until Sunday when my mother told me how bad I looked voicing her concerns. She worked for a Family Medicine doctor, so she went to her office and picked up a few things. My blood pressure was 170/110, the O2 sat 99% and the H&H was coming up at 6/24.

That Sunday evening I called the doctor to report my blood pressure and told him of my other symptoms. He had me come to the ED. I was assessed with an ECHO, chest x-ray and blood work which bought me an ICU bed. I was given a Dobutamine drip which made my headache ten times worse. I could a feel a blood vessel in by head pulsating; I knew it was going to blow.

The Dobutamine was discontinued and I was given Magnesium Sulfate, Demadex and Lovenox. Once I began getting rid of the excess fluid, I felt so much better. After a much improved echocardiogram, I was discharged on Tuesday.

Wednesday morning I weighed myself. I had lost twenty-five pounds in three days. I felt like a new woman. It was a quick turnaround to this cardiomyopathy. Years later, I was evaluated by a Perinatologist that thought I did not have a true cardiomyopathy because of the quick resolution of the disease. I have one healthy child and made it through this ordeal without any permanent heart damage. That is my story, my pregnancy was cursed, but I am blessed with my healthy boy.

୬୬୶

My name is Linda, RN and I have the nurse curse. My story begins with my first pregnancy. I did well until the thirty-two week mark when I went into preterm labor. I was admitted to the hospital and given Mag Sulfate which stopped my labor, but I felt like I had been run over by a truck. I was discharged on bed rest with a T-pump that made me jittery, but kept my contractions away. It was discontinued at thirty-seven weeks and I delivered at thirty-eight weeks.

The curse raised its ugly head again with my second pregnancy. At ten to twelve weeks I noticed a bulge in my lower right side, which was diagnosed as an inguinal hernia. At eighteen weeks I had the hernia repaired under local anesthesia using some sort of mesh. After a six-week recovery, I returned to work and at thirty-two weeks, *then* my left side herniated. I had my baby at thirty-six weeks and the second hernia repaired six weeks later. That was it for me with having babies. But the curse continued.

After these two vaginal births, I was bothered with urinary incontinence and opted to have it surgically repaired using a sling to correct the problem. Only a few hours after my surgery, I was ambulating in my home when I tripped and fell, tearing the repair causing me much pain and agony. I had to have yet another surgery to repair that damage. I plan on no more babies and no more surgeries.

∂∽∾

My name is Kristy and I had the nurse curse. I'm an OB Case Manager and review charts for high risk OB patients. Little did I know that I would have to have my own chart reviewed. On February 19th (my day off) I took my three-year-old to Mother's Day Out. I then went to get my haircut and ran errands until time to pick up my son. My last stop was getting stamps at the post office. As I was standing in line I started to feel a trickle.

I thought, surely I have not peed on myself in public. I tried to act normal thinking I could get out of this line and get to the car before anyone noticed. I ran home and thought that I could change things; praying this was a fluke thing. But, no. It just continued and I knew I was in trouble. I called my mother to run get my three-year-old and made my way to the hospital. I called my doctor who I'd seen two days prior. He arrived shortly after I got to the OB triage area. Yep, my water broke at thirty-two weeks.

When I rolled down to my antepartum unit I was greeted by one of my best nurse friends. After I was somewhat settled and monitored, my nurse came in to tell me I was contracting every two-to-three minutes. *You are kidding me.*

I then was told the dreaded news that I was going to be put on IV Mag Sulfate to try and stop my labor. I'd always heard how awful that medicine made a person feel and unfortunately I was about to find out first hand. Of course, that also meant a Foley catheter to go along with it. *Ugh.* This was not supposed to happen. I was supposed to continue working until my scheduled C-section and then go in to deliver my sweet baby boy, and roll out the front door with my baby in my arms.

I was started on Mag on Friday and stayed on it until Monday. I can remember not being able to even watch TV because I had blurred vision. I remember feeling horrible. It was strange. I started to feel somewhat normal after the med was stopped, but then stayed on bed rest for nineteen more days until on March 7th; Baby Carson decided it was time to be born. Carson was born at thirty-four weeks and four days weighing in at five pounds three ounces. He remained in the NICU for ten days before being able to go home.

As I lay in bed for nineteen days I soon began to realize that God is in control. No matter how much you think you can plan everything, it's really not up to us. I think that God also wanted to make me more sympathetic to the patients. Now, I'm truly able to tell my patients that I know how they feel.

$\approx$

About an hour after I had enjoyed a birthday dinner of fried catfish and all the trimmings, I began to have pain in my right upper quadrant radiating to my back. It was like a knife stabbing me and I splinted the pain by pushing my back against a wall. Oh yeah, I knew what it was. A gallbladder attack. Days later my GYN had his ultrasound girl do a quick scan and there they were little pebbles in my gallbladder. Those are the kinds that cause pancreatitis, I wanted them out.

I asked the CRNAs and the nurses I work with what surgeon I should see. They gave me his name, I had an evaluation, and scheduled my lap chole.

One of my CRNA friends put me to sleep. After I awoke enough for her to talk to me she said "you vagaled to nothing when they put the gas in."

What?

"I was quick to give you some Robinul to bring you out of it. You're fine now," she said.

The next thing I knew, the nurses were stuffing me into my car with a ginger ale in one hand and soda crackers in the other. When I went for my follow up appointment, the surgeon said, "Mrs. Mason, I hope I never have to operate on you again."

"Why?" I asked.

"I didn't like looking up on that monitor and seeing that flat line!"

Nurse Curse.

❧

I plan to write a second book, entitled *The Nurse Curse*. If you are a nurse and want to share your nurse curse story in my book send it to camillemason@centurylink.net for publication.

Common Terms Then and Now

Administrator-----CEO

Afterbirth-----Placenta

Ampicillin -----Amp

Anesthesiologist ---------MDA

Blood clot------DVT

Brethine-----Terb

Cancer------CA

Central Supply-----Materials Management

Cervical check-----SVE

Cesarean Section------C/Section-------Section

Cholecysectomy-----Lap chole

CPR-----BLS

Delalutin -----Makena

Dietary-----Nutrition-----Food Services

Diprivan----- Dip

Director of Nursing-----DON-----CNO

Discharge planning-----Case Management

Doctors------Physicians-----Providers

Doctor's orders-----Physician's orders-----C-POE

Drug Store-----Pharmacy

Elastic stockings-----TEDS

Electric cautery -----Bovie

Electrocardiogram-----ECG-----EKG

Emergency Room-----ER-----ED

Emphysema-----COPD

Enlarged prostate-----BPH

Episiotomy-----Epis

Forceps-----Spoons

Gravida-----G

Gastrostomy tube-----G tube

General anesthesia-----Sleep them

Gentamycin-----Gent

German measles-----Rubella

GI Lab-----Butt Hutt

Gonorrhea-----Clap-----GC

Guaiac test------Hemoccult test

Head nurse-----Charge nurse-----Shift supervisor

Heart attack-----MI

Heart dropsy-----Heart failure-----CHF

Helix-----Fetal scalp electrode-----FSE

Housekeeping-----Environmental services

Hyperstim-----Tachysystole

Hypertension-----HTN

IDDM-----Type I Diabetes

Laceration-----Lac

Linen savers-----Chux

LGA-----Macrosomia

Magnesium Sulfate-----Mag Sulfate-----Mag

Maintenance-----Engineering

MAR-----EMAR

Meconium-----Mec

Medical Records-----Health Information Services

Medical Social Worker-----Case Management

Midwife----CNM

Neonatal Intensive Care Unit-----NICU----- NIC-U-----NI

NIDDM-----Type II Diabetes

No CPR-----No code-----DNR-----AND

Nurse anesthetist-----CRNA.

Nurse clinicians-----Nurse practitioner-----NP

Nurse's aide-----CNA-----Tech

Nursery-----Well baby

Obstetrics-----OB-----Maternal Child Health

Operator-----Switchboard-----PBX

Orderly-----Male attendant

Oxygen-----O2

Oxygen tank-----Oxygen cylinder

Para-----P

Patients-----Clients

Physical therapy-----PT

Piles-----Hemorrhoids

Pitocin-----Pit

Premature rupture of membranes-----PROM

Pulse oximeter-----Pulse ox-----O2 sat monitor

Pyelonephritis-----Pyelo

Recovery Room-----PAC-U

Reflexes-----DTRs

Respiratory therapy-----Respiratory

Rheumatoid arthritis-----RA

Ruptured membranes-----ROM

SGA-----IUGR

Sickle cell patient----Sickler

State board exam-----NCLEX

Stillborn-----IUFD

Telemetry-----Tele

Toxemia of pregnancy-----Preeclampsia

Tracheostomy-----Trach

Unit supervisor-----Unit Manager

Vaginal hysterectomy-----Vag hys

Verineal disease-----VD-----STD

Walk in-----Unattached

Ward Clerk-----Unit Secretary----Unit Clerk

Yellow jaundice-----jaundice

NURSES IN WHITE

You've never seen such an impressive site
When the nurses on duty were dressed in white,
Uniforms starched and ironed just so,
Shoes polished carefully to an immaculate glow.

Caps were pinned securely in place;
Every hair was up and out of our face.
Displayed on our collars, our pins with pride,
Our schools and its teachings we did abide.

With honor and dedication we performed our tasks.
We knew what to do, no questions asked.
We urgently heeded the Code 10 call,
Highly skilled and confident one and all.

Doctors wrote each order with care.
To carry them out, we were always there.
A backrub, a touch, a listening ear,
We won patients' trust and calmed their fear.

Technology and ideas have changed our past,
But the nurse in white will forever last.
In the pages of history, there we will be
For all generations of nurses to see.

Camille Foshee-Mason RN

HAPPY NURSES DAY - MAY 6

196